CAMBRIDGE LIBRARY COLLECTION

Books of enduring scholarly value

Printing and Publishing History

The interface between authors and their readers is a fascinating subject in its own right, revealing a great deal about social attitudes, technological progress, aesthetic values, fashionable interests, political positions, economic constraints, and individual personalities. This part of the Cambridge Library Collection reissues classic studies in the area of printing and publishing history that shed light on developments in typography and book design, printing and binding, the rise and fall of publishing houses and periodicals, and the roles of authors and illustrators. It documents the ebb and flow of the book trade supplying a wide range of customers with products from almanacs to novels, bibles to erotica, and poetry to statistics.

Catalogue of the Valuable Library of the Late Rev. Henry Richards Luard

The academic, university administrator and clergyman Henry Richards Luard (1825–91) graduated from Trinity College, Cambridge, in 1847. He became a fellow and lecturer for several years before his ordination. From 1860 to 1887 he served as vicar of Great St Mary's, and from 1862 until his death he acted as registrary of the university, an increasingly important role during a period of rapid expansion. In addition to these duties, Luard made significant contributions to scholarship. As well as writing for the *Dictionary of National Biography* and editing the work of the classicist Richard Porson, he prepared for the Rolls Series a number of volumes of important medieval texts (which are also reissued in the Cambridge Library Collection). Following his death, the sale of his considerable private library in 1891 took four days, comprising 1,366 lots. This catalogue reveals the sheer breadth of interests for which Victorian scholars of his ilk were noted.

T0352296

Cambridge University Press has long been a pioneer in the reissuing of out-of-print titles from its own backlist, producing digital reprints of books that are still sought after by scholars and students but could not be reprinted economically using traditional technology. The Cambridge Library Collection extends this activity to a wider range of books which are still of importance to researchers and professionals, either for the source material they contain, or as landmarks in the history of their academic discipline.

Drawing from the world-renowned collections in the Cambridge University Library and other partner libraries, and guided by the advice of experts in each subject area, Cambridge University Press is using state-of-the-art scanning machines in its own Printing House to capture the content of each book selected for inclusion. The files are processed to give a consistently clear, crisp image, and the books finished to the high quality standard for which the Press is recognised around the world. The latest print-on-demand technology ensures that the books will remain available indefinitely, and that orders for single or multiple copies can quickly be supplied.

The Cambridge Library Collection brings back to life books of enduring scholarly value (including out-of-copyright works originally issued by other publishers) across a wide range of disciplines in the humanities and social sciences and in science and technology.

Catalogue of the Valuable Library of the Late Rev. Henry Richards Luard

Anonymous

CAMBRIDGE UNIVERSITY PRESS

Cambridge, New York, Melbourne, Madrid, Cape Town,
Singapore, São Paolo, Delhi, Mexico City

Published in the United States of America by Cambridge University Press, New York

www.cambridge.org
Information on this title: www.cambridge.org/9781108057295

© in this compilation Cambridge University Press 2013

This edition first published 1891
This digitally printed version 2013

ISBN 978-1-108-05729-5 Paperback

This book reproduces the text of the original edition. The content and language reflect
the beliefs, practices and terminology of their time, and have not been updated.

Cambridge University Press wishes to make clear that the book, unless originally published
by Cambridge, is not being republished by, in association or collaboration with, or
with the endorsement or approval of, the original publisher or its successors in title.

SOTHEBY, WILKINSON & HODGE'
13, WELLINGTON STREET, STRAND, LONDON.

CATALOGUE

OF THE

VALUABLE LIBRARY

OF THE LATE

REV. HENRY RICHARDS LUARD, D.D.

*Registrary of Cambridge University, Senior Fellow of Trinity
College, and Author or Editor of various Works.*

Days of Sale.

First Day ...	Monday, 16th November ...	Lots	1 to	339
Second Day...	Tuesday, 17th November ...	Lots	340 to	696
Third Day ...	Wednesday, 18th November	Lots	697 to	1033
Fourth Day.	Thursday, 19th November	Lots	1034 to	1366

1891.

CATALOGUE

OF THE

VALUABLE LIBRARY

OF THE LATE

REV. HENRY RICHARDS LUARD, D.D.

Registrary of Cambridge University, Senior Fellow of Trinity College, and Author or Editor of various Works,

COMPRISING

Bibles, Liturgies, Biblical and Liturgical Literature;

ENGLISH & FOREIGN DIVINITY;

GREEK & LATIN CLASSICS (CHIEFLY ON LARGE PAPER)

INCLUDING

FIRST EDITIONS OF HOMER, WELLS' XENOPHON, ROBINSON'S HESIOD, &c.

CHOICE BOOKS OF PRINTS;

Works of Cambridge & Oxford Scholars,

(Many Presentation Copies, with Autograph Letters and Inscriptions);

MATHEMATICAL & SCIENTIFIC PUBLICATIONS;

TRANSACTIONS OF LEARNED SOCIETIES;

CHRONICLES OF GREAT BRITAIN,

published by order of the Master of the Rolls;

COLLECTIONS PRINTED BY GALE AND FELL, SAVILLE, HEARNE, SPARKE, TWYSDEN, WHARTON, and others;

BOOKS RELATING TO CAMBRIDGE UNIVERSITY AND COUNTY,

(Including BENTLEY'S WORKS AND BENTLEYANA);

PUBLICATIONS BY THE ROXBURGHE CLUB,

And of Camden, Early Text and Surtees Societies, &c.

REVIEWS AND MAGAZINES;

And Standard Works in all Classes of Literature.

WHICH WILL BE SOLD BY AUCTION

(By Order of the Executors)

BY MESSRS.

SOTHEBY, WILKINSON & HODGE,

Auctioneers of Literary Property & Works illustrative of the Fine Arts,

AT THEIR HOUSE, No. 13, WELLINGTON STREET, STRAND, W.C.

On MONDAY, 16th NOVEMBER, 1891, and Three following Days,

AT ONE O'CLOCK PRECISELY.

May be Viewed Two Days prior. Catalogues may be had.

DRYDEN PRESS: J. DAVY & SONS, 137, Long Acre, London.

CONDITIONS OF SALE.

I. The highest bidder to be the buyer; and if any dispute arise between bidders, the lot so disputed shall be immediately put up again, provided the Auctioneer cannot decide the said dispute.

II. No person to advance less than 1s.; above five pounds, 2s. 6d.; and so on in proportion.

III. In the case of lots upon which there is a reserve, the Auctioneer shall have the right to bid on behalf of the Seller.

IV. The purchasers to give in their names and places of abode, and to pay down 10s. in the pound, if required, in part payment of the purchase-money; in default of which the lot or lots purchased to be immediately put up again and re-sold.

V. The lots to be taken away, at the buyer's expense immediately after the conclusion of the sale; in default of which Messrs. SOTHEBY, WILKINSON & HODGE will not hold themselves responsible if lost, stolen, damaged, or otherwise destroyed, but they will be left at the sole risk of the purchaser. If, at the expiration of ONE WEEK after the conclusion of the sale the books or other property are not cleared or paid for, they will then be catalogued for immediate sale, and the expense, the same as if re-sold, will be added to the amount at which the books were bought. Messrs. SOTHEBY, WILKINSON & HODGE will have the option of reselling the lots uncleared either by public or private sale without any notice being given to the defaulter.

VI. All the books are presumed to be perfect, unless otherwise expressed; but if upon collating, any should prove defective, the purchaser will be at liberty to take or reject them, provided they are returned within ONE WEEK after the conclusion of the sale, when the purchase-money will be returned.

VII. The sale of any book or books is not to be set aside on account of any worm-holes, stained or short leaves of text or plates, want of list of plates, or blank leaves, or on account of the publication of any subsequent volume, supplement, appendix, or plates. All the manuscripts, autographs, all magazines and reviews, all books in lots, and all tracts in lots or volumes, will be sold with all faults, imperfections and errors of description. The sale of any illustrated book, lot of prints or drawings is not to be set aside on account of any error in the enumeration of the numbers stated, or error of description.

VIII. No IMPERFECT BOOK will be taken back, unless a note accompanies each book, stating its imperfections, with the number of lot and date of the sale at which the same was purchased.

IX. To prevent inaccuracy in the delivery, and inconvenience in the settlement of the purchases, no lot on any account can be removed during the time of sale.

X. Upon failure of complying with the above conditions, the money required and deposited in part of payment shall be forfeited; and *if any loss is sustained in the reselling of such lots as are not cleared or paid for, all charges on such re-sale shall be made good by the defaulters at this sale.*

Gentlemen who cannot attend the Sale may have their Commissions faithfully executed by their humble servants,

SOTHEBY, WILKINSON & HODGE,

13, Wellington Street, Strand.

CATALOGUE

OF THE

VALUABLE LIBRARY

OF THE LATE

REV. HENRY RICHARDS LUARD, D.D.

Registrary of Cambridge University, and Author or Editor of various Works.

FIRST DAY'S SALE.

OCTAVO ET INFRA.

LOT

1 Abercrombie (J.) on Moral Feelings and Intellectual Powers, 2 vol. *half calf gilt*, 1836-37—Bacon (Lord) Harmony of the Essays, &c. arranged by E. Arber, 1871—Sharp (R.) Letters and Essays, 1834 (4)

2 Æschyli Tragœdiæ cum Scholiis, Græce, cura F. Robortelli, 2 vol. in 1, *russia extra, gilt edges*   *Venetiis*, 1552
*** Scarce. The Scholia only, sold for £2 12s. in Sir M. Sykes's sale.

3 Æschyli Tragœdiæ, Græce, FIRST EDITION, *Duke of Sussex's copy, russia extra, gilt gaufré edges, Venetiis, Aldus,* 1518
*** Very rare. Sir J. Thorold's copy sold for £11.

4 Æschyli Tragœdiæ, Græce, *very large and fine copy in French red morocco, gilt edges, Paris. A. Turnebus,* 1552

5 Æschyli Opera Gr. cum Commentario F. A. Paley, 2 vol. *editor's autograph letter added, calf extra, Cantab.* 1847

6 Æschyli, Prometheus Vinctus ; Choephoræ ; Septem contra Thebas ; Persæ et Agamemnon, Græce, cum Notis et Glossariis C. J. Blomfield, 5 vol. 1839-34-24-40-26— Eumenides in Greek with critical Remarks by C. O. Müller, *Camb.* 1835—Supplices, Gr. cum Notis A. Wellauer. Accedunt Fragmenta et Scholia Græca, *Cantab.* 1827—Beatson (B. W.) Index Græcitatis Æschyleæ, *ib.* 1830, *calf gilt*   8 vol.

B

7 Æschylus Gr. ex Recensione F. A. Paley, *Cantab*. 1858—
Æschylus in English with Notes, *illustrations by Flaxman*, 1831—Agamemnon, translated by W. Sewell,
1846—Æschylus literally translated by T. A. Buckley,
bust, 1849 (4)

8 Æsopicarum Fabularum Delectus Gr. et Lat. edente A. Al-
sop, LARGE PAPER, *frontispiece, old calf, Oxoniæ*, 1698
** Scarce on large paper. Col. Stanley's copy sold for
£2 18s.

9 Agostino (Santo) della Città di Dio : Volgarizzamento del
buon Secolo ridotto alla vera Lezione da O. Gigli, 9 vol.
*red morocco extra, gilt edges, with arms of Cardinal
Asquini in gold on sides* *Roma*, 1842

10 Aikin (J.) The Athenæum from January 1807 to June
1809 inclusive, 30 *nos.* in 5 *vol. with the original covers,
half bound, uncut* 1807-9

11 Alani (H.) Observationes in Ciceronem, &c. *Dublinii*, 1863;
with 5 other Works by Alan and Paley on Quintus
Smyrnæus and J. H. Smith on Coincidences in Thucydides and Acts in the Volume, *half calf gilt*

12 Alciphron's Epistles describing domestic Manners, Courte-
sans and Parasites of Greece (translated by W. Beloe
and T. Monro), *see MS. notes on fly-leaves, tree-marbled
calf extra* 1791

13 Aldhelmi (S.) Opera edidit J. A. Giles *Oxonii*, 1841

14 Alford (H.) Earnest Dissuasive from joining the Church of
Rome, 1846, and 21 other Theological and Miscellaneous
Tracts in the Volume, *half calf gilt* 1846-58

15 Alison (Sir A.) History of Europe from 1789 to 1815,
20 vol. *portrait, cloth* *Edinb.* 1847-48

16 Ampère (J. J.) Histoire Romaine à Rome, 4 vol. *Paris*,
1872—L'Empire Romain à Rome, 2 vol. *ib.* 1872, *gilt
vellum* 6 *vol.*

17 Analecta Veterum Poetarum Græcorum Editore R. F. P.
Brunck, 3 vol. *panelled calf extra, Argentorati*, 1772-76

18 Anderson (J. P.) Book of British Topography in the
British Museum 1881

19 Anglo-Saxon Legends of St. Andrew and St. Veronica in
Anglo-Saxon and English, by C. W. Goodwin, *Cambridge*, 1851—Babington (C. D.) Ancient Cambridgeshire, *map and plan*, 1853—Reed (E.) Diary (1709-20)
with unpublished Letters of Dr. Bentley, edited by
H. R. Luard, *ib.* 1860—Porson (R.) Correspondence,
edited by H. R. Luard, *ib.* 1867—Sandars (S.) Notes
on Great St. Mary's Church, with Annals of the Church
by Canon Venables, *woodcuts, ib.* 1869, *half red morocco, uncut, top edge gilt* *in* 1 *vol.*

20 Anwitti (V.) Evangeli delle Domeniche, *half vellum, Roma,*
  1879—Évangiles traduites par H. Laserre, *Paris,* 1887
  —Renan (E.) Vie de Jésus, *Leipzig,* 1863; and 2 small
  English Testaments (5)
21 Annals of England, 3 vol. *woodcuts* *Oxford,* 1857-58
22 Annales de l'Abbaye d'Aiguibelle de l'Ordre de Citeaux
  (Congrégation de N. D. de la Trappe), par un Religieux
  de ce Monastère, 2 vol. *views, half vellum, uncut*
  Valence, 1863
23 ANTE-NICENE CHRISTIAN LIBRARY, 24 vol. *Edinb.* 1867-72
24 Anthologia Græca, *vellum* *Venetiis, Aldus,* 1550-51
  ⁎ Third and best Aldine Edition. Sir J. Thorold's copy
  sold for £4.
25 Apocryphal Acts of the Apostles in Syriac and English, by
  W. Wright, 2 vol. 1871
26 Apolinarii Interpretatio Psalmorum Versibus heroicis,
  Græce, FIRST EDITION, *Cardinal Richelieu's copy, with
  his arms in gold preserved pasted inside the cover, red
  morocco, gilt edges* *Paris. A. Turnebus,* 1552
  ⁎ Rare. Sir J. Thorold's copy sold for £1 18s.
27 APOLLONII RHODII ARGONAUTICA, cum Scholiis, Græce,
  olive morocco extra, gilt edges *Venetiis, Aldus,* 1521
  ⁎ Very scarce. Mr. Beckford's copy sold for £9 15s. and
  Sir J. Thorold's for £9.
28 Apostolic Fathers, viz. Clement of Rome (St.) Two Epistles
  to the Corinthians ; S. Ignatius and S. Polycarp, in
  Greek and English, with Introductions, Notes and Dissertations by Bp. J. B. Lightfoot, 5 vol. *with Editor's
  autograph inscriptions* *Cambridge,* 1869-85
29 Apparizione della B. Vergine a due Pastorelli sul Monte
  della Salette, *frontispiece, Monza,* 1852—Via Crucis da
  S. Leonardo da Porto Maurizio, *plates, Roma,* 1859 ;
  and other Tracts in the Volume
30 Apthorp (G. F.) Catalogue of Books and Manuscripts in
  Lincoln Cathedral Library *Lincoln,* 1859
31 Apuleii Opera. Accedit Alcinoi Isagoge Platonicæ Philo-
  sophiæ, Græce *Venetiis, Aldus,* 1521
  ⁎ Scarce. Sir J. Thorold's copy sold for £1 16s.
32 Aristæneti Epistolæ Gr. et Lat. cum Notis, *autograph notes
  and book-plate of Bp. C. J. Blomfield, old red morocco*
  Paris. 1594
33 Aristophanis Thesmophoriazusæ et Lysistrate, Græce,
  stained, half morocco *Florentiæ, B. Junta,* 1515
34 Aristophanis Acharnenses, Græce, cum Notis P. Elmsley,
  russia extra, gilt edges *Oxonii,* 1809
  ⁎ Very scarce, having been rigidly suppressed by Elmsley,
  who had used Porson's hints without permission.

35 Aristophanes Comedies translated by T. Mitchell, 2 vol.
    in 1, *calf*   1820-22

36 Aristophanis Comœdiæ et Fragmenta Græce ex Recensione
    G. Dindorfii cum Scholiis Græcis et Indice Aristophanico
    J. Caravellæ, 8 vol. *calf extra*   *Oxonii*, 1838

37 Aristophanis Comœdiæ XI Græce cum Notulis H. A.
    Holden, *numerous MS. notes by H. R. Luard, who has
    added an autograph letter of the Editor, uncut*   1848

38 Aristotle on the Constitution of Athens, in Greek, edited
    by F. G. Kenyon   *Oxford*, 1891

39 Arnold (M.) New Poems, *brown morocco extra, gilt edges*
                                                  1867

40 Arnold (T.) Sermons on Christian Life   1844

41 Arnold (T.) Introductory Lectures on Modern History 1845

42 Arrivabene (F.) Il Secolo di Dante colle Illustrazioni
    storiche di Ugo Foscolo sul Poema di Dante, *Monza*,
    1858—Puecher-Passavolli (I.) Viaggio da Dosenzano a
    Trento, *map and views, Milano*, 1844   *in 1 vol.*

43 Arsenii Archiepiscopi Monembasiæ Præclara Dicta Philo-
    sophorum, Imperatorum, Oratorumque et Poetarum,
    Græce, *morocco, s. a.*—Dialogus Studiosi Bibliopolæ et
    Libri; Porphyrius de Plagiis Philosophorum et Rhetorum,
    &c. Græce, *vellum, ib. s. a.*   (2)

44 Athenæus, Græce ex Recensione G. Dindorfii, 3 vol. *half
    red morocco extra*   *Lipsiæ*, 1827

45 Atti della R. Società Romana di Storia Patria (1884-90)
    10 Nos. (*wanting No. 8*)   *Roma*, 1885-90

46 Auctores Classici Latini, 39 vol. REGENT'S EDITION, *calf
    gilt*   1815-30

47 AUGUSTINE (SAINT) WORKS, a new Translation, edited
    by Rev. M. Dods, 15 vol. *cloth*   *Edinb.* 1871-76

48 Auli Gellii Noctes Atticæ cum Notis J. F. Gronovii, *fine
    copy in red morocco extra, gilt edges, by J. Clarke*
                               Lugd. Bat. 1687

   ⁎ A MS. Note describes this copy as on Large Paper and
    unique.

49 Aulus Gellius, Attic Nights, translated by Rev. W. Beloe,
    3 vol. *old calf extra*   1795

50 Austen (Jane) Emma, 3 vol. FIRST EDITION, 1816—Mac-
    kenzie (H.) Man of Feeling, *frontispiece*, 1781—Dumas
    (A.) George, *Belfast*, 1846—Goldsmith (O.) Citizen
    of the World, 2 vol. *portrait and plates*, 1809—Gold-
    smith (O.) Essays and Poems, *frontispiece and vignette
    title*, 1836   (8)

51 Avrillon (M.) Guide for passing Advent and Lent holily and Year of Affections, with Prefaces by E. B. Pusey, 3 vol. 1847—Maclear (G. F.) Class-Book of the Catechism, *Camb.* 1868—Mill (W. H.) Lectures on the Catechism, *ib.* 1856—Maclear (G. F.) Hour of Sorrow, *autograph letter of Author added, ib.* 1875—Littledale (R. F.) Plain Reason against joining the Church of Rome, *author's autograph letter,* 1880　　　　　　(7)

52 Ayscough (S.) Index to Shakspeare, *vellum extra*　　1827

53 Aytoun (W. E.) Lays of the Scottish Cavaliers and other Poems, *Edinb.* 1854—Procter (Adelaide Anne) Legends and Lyrics, 2 vol. 1860-61—Moore (T.) Poetical Works, *illustrations by F. Gilbert,* 1873—Calverley (C. S.) Fly Leaves, *Camb.* 1872—Goethe (J. W. von) Poems and Ballads, translated by W. E. Aytoun and Sir T. Martin, *Edinb.* 1859　　　　　　(6)

54 Babington (C.) Influence of Christianity in the Abolition of Slavery, *Cambridge,* 1846—Lord Macaulay's Character of the Clergy considered, *ib.* 1849—Hyperides Funeral Oration over Leosthenes and Comrades in Greek, with Notes by C. Babington, *ib.* 1859—Lecture on Archæology, *ib.* 1865　　　　　　(4)

55 Babrii Fabulæ Æsopiæ Græce edente G. C. Lewis, 2 Parts in 1, FIRST EDITION *of Part II, half russia, Oxonii,* 1846-59

56 Bailey (H.) Rituale Anglo-Catholicum, 1847—Mackenzie (H.) Christian Clergy of the first ten Centuries, *Camb.* 1853—Neale (J. M.) Mediæval Preachers and Mediæval Preaching, 1856—Copy of Alterations in the Book of Common Prayer in 1689, 1854　　　　　　(4)

57 Bailey (J. E.) Life of T. Fuller, *portraits and plates*　1874

58 Baillie (Joanna) Dramatic and Poetical Works, *portrait and vignette title*　　　　　　1851

59 Ball (W. W. Rouse) History of the Study of Mathematics at Cambridge, *with autograph letter of Author added, Camb.* 1889—Ingleby (C. M.) on the Revival of Philosophy at Cambridge, *ib.* 1870—Monk (Bp. J. H.) Cambridge Classical Examinations, *ib.* 1826　　　(3)

60 Balzani (U.) Early Chronicles of Italy, 1883—Sismondi (J. C. L. de) Italian Republics, 1832—Murray, Jameson and Wilson's Africa, *map, plans and plates, Edinb.* 1832 — Russell (M.) Egypt, *map and plates, ib.* 1832 —Goldsmith (O.) Roman History abridged, 2 vol. *Leghorn,* 1815　　　　　　(6)

61 Barker (E. H.) Parriana or Notices of the Rev. S. Parr, LL.D. 2 vol. *half calf gilt*　　　　　　1828-29

62 Barker (E. H.) Literary Anecdotes, 2 vol. *with Autograph Note of J. Hunter stating this is one of the five only uncastrated copies*　　　　　　1852

63 Barker (E. H.) Legitimacy of R. Barker, *only 50 copies printed, Leeds,* 1822—Letter in the Cause of the Greeks, 1823 ; and other Tracts by Barker in the Volume, *with Author's autograph inscriptions and long holograph letter to Archdeacon Wrangham, half bound, uncut*

64 Baker (T.) History of the College of St. John the Evangelist, Cambridge, edited by J. E. B. Mayor, 2 vol. *with autograph letter of the Editor added, half red morocco*
Cambridge, 1869

65 Barri (G.) Painter's Voyage of Italy, translated by W. Lodge, *etchings by Lodge with his portrait added, calf extra* 1679

66 Barrow (I.) Works, with Life by Rev. J. Hamilton, 3 vol. *portrait* *Edinb.* 1841

67 Barrow (I.) Mathematical Works, edited by W. Whewell
Cambridge, 1860

68 Bartholomæi, de Cotton Historia Anglicana (449-1298) et Liber de Archiepiscopis et Episcopis Angliæ, edited by H. R. Luard, *half calf extra* 1859

69 Bartlett (W. H.) Walks about Jerusalem, *plan and plates* 1844

70 Bayard (Chevalier) Feats, Gests and Prowesses by the Loyal Servant, 2 vol. *calf extra* 1825

71 Beckington (Bp. T.) Embassy to negociate a Marriage between Henry VI and a Daughter of the Count of Armagnac, with Notes by Sir N. H. Nicolas
W. Pickering, 1828

72 Beaconsfield (B. Disraeli, Earl of) Coningsby, *port.* 1849—Sybil, *half calf extra, Leipzig,* 1845 — Endymion, Lothair and Vivian Grey, 3 vol. *n. d.* (5)

73 Beeton's Dictionary of Universal Information, *maps, &c. half calf, m. e.* *n. d.*

74 Bellendenus (G.) de Statu cum Præfatione S. Parr, 3 *portraits and 2 plates, Bp. C. J. Blomfield's copy, with his book-plate and MS. notes, calf* 1787

75 Bellows (A. J.) Philosophy of Eating, 1869 — Richardson (B. W.) on Health and Occupation, 1879 (2)

76 Beloe (W.) Poems and Translations, *half calf* 1788

77 Beloe (W.) Miscellanies, 3 vol. *calf* 1795

78 Beloe (W.) Anecdotes of Literature and scarce Books, 6 vol. *tree-marbled calf extra, uncut, top edges gilt, by Cecil and Larkins* 1807-12

79 Beloe (W.) Sexagenarian, 2 vol. *MS. notes by Mr. Beckford (4 pages) and numerous by H. R. Luard, with autograph letter of Beloe added, half russia* 1807
 ⁎⁎⁎ This copy sold for £2 2s. in Mr. Beckford's sale, since which Dr. Luard has made a Key to the names and numerous MS. Notes.

80 Bentley. Articles against Bentley, 1710—Present State of Trinity College by Dr. Bentley, 1710 ; and 7 other Tracts relating to Trinity College in the volume, *half calf gilt* 1710-11

81 Bentley. Boyle (Hon. C.) Examination of Bentley's Phalaris, 1699—Short Account of Bentley's Humanity and Justice, 1699—Johnson (R.) Aristarchus Anti-Bentleianus, *Nottinghamiæ*, 1717—Ciceronis Tusculanæ Disputationes cum Commentario J. Davisii et R. Bentleii Emendationibus, *Cantab.* 1738 — Review of Bentley's Emendations of Milton, *half calf gilt*, 1732—Horace, in Latin and English, with Translation of Bentley's Notes (by Oldisworth). To which are added Notes upon Notes, 24 parts in 2 vol. 1713 (7)

82 Bentley. Ciceronis Tusculanæ Disputationes cum Commentario J. Davisii et R. Bentleii Emendationibus, LARGE PAPER, *russia extra, gilt edges* *Oxonii*, 1805

83 Bentley (R.) Emendationes in Plautum, 1880—Epistola ad J. Millium, *half calf gilt* — Review of Proceedings against Dr. Bentley, 1719 — Animadversions on the Proceedings, 1722 — Reflections on the Aspersions cast on the Clergy, 1717—Review of Bentley's Emendations of Milton, 1732 (6)

84 Bentley. Present State of Trinity College, 1716 — Miller (E.) Cambridge and its Colleges, 1717 — Letter to Bentley on his Greek Testament, 1717—Middleton (C.) Account of Proceedings against Dr. Bentley, 2 parts, 1719, *half calf gilt* *in* 1 *vol.* 1716-19

85 Bentley (R.) Works, collected and edited by Rev. A. Dyce, 3 vol. *autograph letter of Dyce added*, 1836-38 — Notæ in Callimachum, *Ultraj.* 1697—Emendationes in Menandrum et Philemonem, *Cantab.* 1714—Present State of Trinity College, 1710, *in* 1 *vol.*—Emendationes in Ciceronis Tusculanas Quæstiones, *Oxon.* 1805 — Annotationes in Lucretium, *Oxon.* 1818—Curæ novissimæ in Horatium —Emendationes in Ovidium, Silium Italicum, Senecam, Nicandrum, Aristophanem, Sophoclem, Theocritum, Bionem et Moschum, &c. *cuttings from other Publications, in* 1 *vol.* — Critica Sacra, edited by A. A. Ellis, *Camb.* 1862—Rud (E.) Diary, with Bentley's unpublished Letters, *ib.* 1860 — Maehly (J.) Biographie von R. Bentley et Anecdota zu Homer, *Leipzig*, 1868, *in* 1 *vol.* — Correspondence, edited by C. Wordsworth, 2 vol. 1842 — Life, by Bp. J. H. Monk, 2 vol. *portrait, autograph letter respecting Bentley from J. E. B. Mayor, with printed letters added*, 1833, *uniform in calf extra* 10 *vol.*

86 Bentley. Menandri et Philemonis Reliquiæ, Gr. et Lat.
cum Notis H. Grotii et J. Clerici, *Amst.* 1709 — Bent-
leii (R.) Emendationes in Menandrum et Philemonem
Traj. ad Rhen. 1710, *in* 1 *vol. MS. Notes, vellum*—
Gronovii (Jacobi) Infamia Emendationum Bentleii in
Menandrum, *calf gilt, extremely rare, Lugd. Bat.* 1710

87 Bentley, by R. C. Jebb, *with author's autograph letter added*
Cambridge, 1882

88 Beresford (J.) Miseries of Human Life, 2 vol. *frontispieces*
and cuts, 1826—Lyly (J.) Euphues Anatomy of Wit
and his England, 1868—Cervantes (M. de) The Squib,
Camb. 1849 ; and 10 others　　　　　　　　(14)

89 Berger (E.) Notice sur Manuscrits de la Bibliothèque Vaticane : Richard le Poitevin, *facsimile, half vellum*
Paris, 1879

90 Bernardi (S.) Opera omnia. Editio Benedictina repetita,
4 vol. *half red morocco*　　　　　　　　　*ib.* 1839

91 Best (H.) Four Years in France, with Account of Author's
Conversion to the Catholic Faith, 2 *pages of autograph*
notes of W. Beckford, calf gilt　　　　　　1826

⁎ This copy sold for £1 10s. in Mr. Beckford's sale.

92 Bibel, Deutsch durch Dr. M. Luther, *calf gilt*
Hannover, 1838

93 Bible (Holy), *pica super royal 8vo edition, blue morocco*
extra, gilt edges　　　　　　　　*Cambridge, n. d.*

94 Bible (Holy), being Revised Versions of the Old and New
Testaments, 5 vol. LARGE PAPER, *cloth, uncut*
ib. 1885 & 1881

95 Bible (Holy), translated by the English College at Doway
and Rhemes, *Belfast,* 1839—Crown of Jesus, *frontis-*
piece, n. d.—Abbott (J.) Young Christian, *n. d.*—Milner
(J.) End of Religious Controversy, *portrait,* 1843 —
Augustine (St.) Confessions, *Oxford,* 1848—Nouveau
Paroissien Romain, *plates, morocco, gilt edges, in case,*
Dijon, 1855 ; and 3 others, Religious　　　　(9)

96 Bible. The English Version of the Polyglott Bible, *morocco,*
gilt edges, with silver clasps, 1833—Children's Hymn
Book, *with Tunes, n. d.*—Hymns, Ancient and Modern,
edited by W. H. Monk, *with Tunes, n. d.*　　　(3)

97 Bible. Book of Common Prayer and New Version of
Psalms, 3 vol. in 1, *morocco, gilt edges, Oxford,* 1845—
Brooks (P.) Candle of the Lord, and other Sermons,
1884—Paley (W.) Horæ Paulinæ and Horæ Apostolicæ,
by T. R. Birks, *map, autograph letter of Birks added,*
1850—Mason (A. J.) Faith of the Gospel, 1888 ; and
8 others, Religious　　　　　　　　　　(12)

98 Bickersteth (E. H.) Yesterday, To-Day and For Ever, a
Poem, *presentation copy, with author's autograph inscription* 1866

99 Bickersteth (E. H.) Christian Student, 1844—Water from
the Well-Spring, 1852, *presentation copies, with author's
autograph inscriptions* (2)

100 Bickersteth (E. H.) Nineveh, and Poems, 2 vol. *with author's
autograph inscriptions,* 1851, *and Camb.* 1849—Emerson
(W.) Papers from my Desk and other Poems, *autograph
letter of J. H. Röhrs added,* 1873—Emerson (W.) The
Critic, 1874—Röhrs (J. H.) Poems, *autograph letter of
author added,* 1848 — Eliot (George) Spanish Gipsy,
Edinb. 1868 — Jones (T. P.) Firmilian, *ib.* 1854—
Campbell (T.) Poetical Works, *portrait, calf extra, ib.*
1837—Dryden (J.) Poetical Works, 3 vol. *frontispieces,
calf gilt,* 1813 — Butler (S.) Poetical Works, 3 vol. *frontispieces, calf gilt,* 1813 (14)

101 Biograph and Review, vol. V, No. 29 and 30—New Series,
vol. I in 4 parts 1881-82

102 Biographical Tracts. Memoir of H. V. Bayley, *printed for
private circulation only,* 1846 ; and 16 other Tracts in
the volume (*see list of contents on fly-leaf*), *half calf gilt*

103 Biography. Nicholas Ferrar, two Lives, by his Brother
John and Dr. Jebb, *Camb.* 1865 —Autobiography of M.
Robinson, *ib.* 1856—Life of Bp. Bedell by his Son, *ib.*
1871—Forbes (A.) Chinese Gordon, 1885—C. G. Gordon,
by R. H. Barnes and C. E. Brown, *facsimile letter,* 1885
— Beesly (A. H.) Sir John Franklin, *map,* 1881—
Selwyn (L. F.) Memorials of four Brothers, *photographs,
Richmond, n. d.* (7)

104 Birch (W. De Gray) Fasti Monastici Ævi Saxonici 1872

105 Birch (W. De Gray) and H. Jenner, Early Drawings and
Illuminations, *plates* 1879

106 Blades (W.) Biography and Typography of W. Caxton,
woodcuts 1882

107 Bland (R.) Collections from the Greek Anthology and
from the Pastoral, Elegiac and Dramatic Poets of
Greece, *calf gilt,* 1813 — Greek Anthology, in Prose, by
G. Burges ; and Metrical Versions by Bland and others,
1852 (2)

108 Blaauw (W. H.) Barons' War, including Battles of Lewes
and Evesham 1871

109 Blomfield (Bp. C. J.) Reviews cut out of Edinburgh and
Quarterly Reviews and Museum Criticum, in 1 vol. *with
autograph letter of Bp. Blomfield, containing List of his
Contributions to Periodicals, half russia*

110 Blomfieldii (C. J. *Episcopi Londinensis*) Opuscula. A
Collection of 28 Cuttings from Museum Criticum and
other Periodicals, *half calf gilt* *in* 1 *vol.*

111 Blunt (J. H.) Directorium Pastorale, 1864—Cope (Sir
W. H.) and H. Stretton, Visitatio Infirmorum, 1854—
Eclipse of Faith, 1855—Nouet (M.) Life of Christ in
Glory, 1847 ; and 9 others, Religious (13)

112 Boccaccio (G.) Il Decameron, 5 vol. *uncastrated edition,*
plates, vellum, uncut *Firenze,* 1830-31

113 Bookworm (The), 3 vol. *in cloth ;* and No. 37 to 42 inclusive 1888-91

114 Borrow (G.) Bible and Gypsies in Spain, 2 vol. 1843-46
—Meyrick (F.) Practical Working of the Church of
Spain, *Oxford,* 1851—Castro (A. de) History of the
Jews in Spain, *Camb.* 1851—Mocatta (F. D.) Jews of
Spain and Portugal and the Inquisition, 1877 (5)

115 Bonwicke (Ambrose) Life by his Father, *Cambridge,* 1870
—Pattern for Young Students in the University set
forth in the Life of A. Bonwicke, *an unfinished work,*
ending with p. 516 (2)

116 Boswell (J.) Life of Dr. S. Johnson, including Tour to
the Hebrides, by Rt. Hon. J. W. Croker, *portraits* 1848

117 Botfield (B.) Notes on Cathedral Libraries of England,
" *From the Author* " 1849
⁎ Privately printed for presents only.

118 Bourne (V.) Poemata Latine partim reddita partim scripta,
calf *Oxonii,* 1826

119 Bowden (J. W.) Life and Pontificate of Gregory VII,
2 vol. *calf gilt* 1840

120 Bowles (W. L.) and J. G. Nichols, Annals and Antiquities of Lacock Abbey, Wilts, *plates, half red morocco*
extra 1835

121 Bracton's Note Book of Cases decided in the King's
Courts during the Reign of Henry III, annotated seem-
ingly by Henry of Bratton, edited by F. W. Maitland,
3 vol. 1887

122 Bradshaw (H.) Skeleton of Chaucer's Canterbury Tales,
Camb. 1868—University Library, *ib.* 1881—Hiber-
nensis Canons, *ib.* 1885 ; and 3 others (6)

123 Bradshaw (H.) Collected Papers, 13 *facsimiles, Camb.*
1889—Life by G. W. Prothero, *portrait, with autograph*
letter of Bradshaw and 2 *autograph letters of Prothero*
added, 1888 (2)

124 Bray (Mrs.) The Borders of the Tamar and the Tavy,
2 vol. *woodcuts* 1879

125 Brathwait (R.) Drunken Barnabee's Journal in Latin and English Jingles, edited by J. Haslewood, *frontispiece*, 1818—Montgomery (J.) Poet's Portfolio, 1835—Smith (J. and H.) Rejected Addresses, *portraits and illustrations by G. Cruikshank*, 1841 ; and 5 others, Poetical (8)

126 Breviarium Romanum, 4 vol. *plates, old black morocco, gilt edges* *Antverpiæ*, 1715

127 Breviarium Romanum Quignonianum curante J. W. Legg, *editor's autograph letter added* *Cantab.* 1888

128 Brewer (J. S.) English Studies 1881

129 Brewer (J. S.) Reign of Henry VIII, 2 vol. *portrait, cloth, uncut* 1884

130 Brewster (Sir D.) Memoirs of Sir I. Newton, 2 vol. *portrait and statue, with woodcuts*, 1855—Gray (G. J.) Bibliography of Newton's Works, *Camb.* 1888 (3)

131 Bristed (C. A.) Five Years in an English University (Cambridge), 2 vol. *New York*, 1852

132 BRITANNICARUM RERUM MEDII ÆVI SCRIPTORES, OR CHRONICLES AND MEMORIALS OF GREAT BRITAIN AND IRELAND DURING THE MIDDLE AGES, published by the Authority of Her Majesty's Treasury under the Direction of the Master of the Rolls, with the cancelled Volume of Royal and Historical Letters, MS. Corrections by H. R. Luard, 232 vol. *numerous facsimiles, half Roxburghe, uncut* 1858-90

*** Several of the works were edited or corrected by Dr. Luard, who has inserted in the volumes autograph letters connected with the publication from T. Arnold ; C. Babington ; E. A. Bond ; H. Bradshaw ; J. S. Brewer ; W. G. Clark ; O. Cockayne ; C. A. Cole ; J. F. Dimock; Sir H. Ellis ; J. Gairdner ; J. Glove ; N. E. S. A. Hamilton ; T. D. Hardy ; W. Hardy; W. H. Hart; F. S. Haydon ; F. C. Hingeston; F. Jourdain; F. Liebermann; J. R. Lumby ; W. D. Macray ; Sir F. Madden ; E. Magnusson; C. T. Martin ; J. Raine ; W. T. Riley ; J. C. Robertson ; W. W. Shirley ; J. Stevenson ; W Stubbs ; and W. B. Turnbull.

133 British Apollo, 3 vol. *frontispiece* 1740

134 Bronte (Emily) Wuthering Heights and Agnes Grey, by Anne Bronte, 1869—Gaskell (Mrs.) Life of Charlotte Bronte, 1869—Poynter (E. Frances) My Little Lady, 2 vol. in 1, *half calf extra, Leipzig*, 1871—Mansfield (R. B) Log of the Water Lily, *half calf extra, ib.* 1854 —Burney (Miss) Evelina, *half calf extra, ib.* 1850— Longfellow (H. W.) Hyperion and Kavanagh, 1852 (6)

135 Brougham (H. Lord) Statesmen of the Time of George III, Three Series, 6 vol. in 3, *cloth, gilt edges* 1845

136 Broughton (Lord) Italy, 2 vol. 1859

137 Brown (Rawdon) Prefaces to Venetian Papers (1202-1533), 4 vol. 1864-71

138 Browning (Robt.) Prince Hohenstiel-Schwangau, FIRST EDITION 1871

139 Browning. Fifine at the Fair, FIRST EDITION 1872

140 Browning. Aristophanes' Apology, FIRST EDITION 1875

141 Browning. Pacchiarotto, FIRST EDITION 1876

142 Browning. Agamemnon of Æschylus, FIRST EDITION 1877

143 Browning. La Saisiaz, FIRST EDITION 1878

144 Brunet (J. C.) Manuel du Libraire et de l'Amateur de Livres, 4 vol. in 1, *blue morocco extra, gilt edges* *Bruxelles*, 1838-39

145 Bryce (J.) Holy Roman Empire, 1871—Sewell (E. M.) and C. M. Yonge, European History, 1873—About (E.) Greece and Greeks of the Present Day, *Edinb.* 1855—Mirabeau's Letters during his Residence in England, 2 vol. *portrait*, 1832—Head (Sir F. B.) The Emigrant, 1847 (6)

146 Buckland (F. T.) Curiosities of Natural History, 2 vol. *frontispieces, cloth* 1886

147 Bull (Bp. G.) Works collected by Rev. E. Burton, D.D. with Life by R. Nelson, 8 vol. *calf extra, presented by A. Compton with his autograph letter added, Oxford*, 1846

148 Bunyan (J.) Pilgrim's Progress, *half Roxburghe, top edge gilt, Cambridge*, 1862—Quarles (F.) Judgment and Mercy for afflicted Souls, *portrait, calf extra*, 1807—Crosthwaite (J. C.) Modern Hagiology, 2 vol. *uncut*, 1846 (4)

149 Burges (G.) Son of Erin, 1823—Nine Classical Criticisms (including Translation of Avis of Sophocles and several in his own handwriting, with autograph letters of his Daughter, A. Snowdon, and W. T. Haworth added, *in 1 vol. half bound*—Æschyli Supplices et Eumenides Græce recensente G. Burges, 2 vol. and 5 pages of MS. Emendations of Æschylus in his handwriting, *with Epigram in Greek and English by G. Burges added*, and MS. Notes by Bp. Blomfield—Translation of Demosthenes' Midian Oration, *Camb.* 1842, *half russia*, 1821-22—Euripidis Bacchæ Gr. edente G. Burges, *half russia*—Euripidis Phœnissæ, Gr. cum Notulis G. Burges, 1809 (6)

150 Burney (C. P.) Monthly Reviews of various Publications, in 1 vol. *calf extra* 1783-1800

151 Burney (C.) de Metris ab Æschylo in choricis Cantibus adhibitis, LARGE PAPER, *russia extra, rough leaves, gilt edges* *Cantab.* 1809

152 Burgon (Dean J. W.) The Revision revised   1883

153 Burgon (J. W.) Letters from Rome, *plates*, 1862—Abbott (J. N.) Sketches of Modern Athens, *presentation copy with author's autograph Greek inscription*, 1849—Dickens (C.) Pictures from Italy, *half calf gilt, Paris*, 1846—Jameson (Mrs.) Diary of an Ennuyée, *half calf gilt*, 1826— Matthews (H.) Diary of an Invalid, *calf*, 1820—Twiss (R.) Trip to Paris, *frontispiece*, 1793   (6)

154 Burns (R.) Poetical Works, 3 vol. *frontispieces*   1823

155 Burton (R.) Anatomy of Melancholy, 2 vol. LARGE PAPER, *frontispieces, old russia*   1800

156 Butler (A.) Lives of the Fathers, Martyrs and other principal Saints, 12 vol. in 4, *portraits, illuminated titles and plates, morocco extra, with cross in gold on sides*
New York, n. d.

157 Butler (Bp. J.) Analogy of Religion, and Sermons, 2 vol.
Oxford, 1844

158 Byrom (J.) Miscellaneous Poems, 2 vol. LARGE PAPER, *portraits and vignettes, old gilt tree-marbled calf*
Manchester, 1773

159 Byron (Lord) Poetical Works, 10 vol. *frontispieces and vignette titles*, 1851—Life with Letters and Journals by T. Moore, 6 vol. *portrait, frontispieces and vignette titles*, 1851   16 *vol.*

160 CÆSARIS COMMENTARII cura Aldi, *large copy, woodcuts and capitals illuminated in gold and colours, " Massilia " and " Uxellodunum " in the autograph of Aldus beneath the cuts, and with his holograph Index, old calf, gilt gaufre edges*   *Venetiis, Aldus*, 1513

   ⁎⁎ On the title-page is motto " Brevis consulendi occasio " and possessor's name " Jacobi Brellii et amicorum." It is the rarest of the Aldine Editions. Sir J. Thorold's copy sold for £21.

161 Cæsaris (C. Julii) Rerum Gestarum Commentarii, *woodcut maps, old morocco gilt, gilt edges*   *Lugd.* 1545

162 Calendarium Genealogicum Henry III and Edward I, edited by C. Roberts, 2 vol. *facsimiles*, 1865—Calendar of the Carew Manuscripts (1575-88) edited by J. S. Brewer and W. Bullen, with Preface to vol. II, 2 vol. 1868   4 *vol.*

163 Callimachi quæ supersunt cum Notis C. J. Blomfield, *calf extra*   1815

164 Cambridge Antiquarian Society's Communications (1850-80), 4 vol. *plates, half red morocco, uncut, top edges gilt*
Cambridge, 1859-81

165 Cambridge. Catalogue of the Manuscripts in the University Library, 4 vol. A–OO), *Camb.* 1856-61—Catalogue Baumgartner and Patrick Papers, Baker Manuscripts, &c. forming vol. V, *ib.* 1867—Index, *ib.* 1867, *with autograph letters of W. H. Bateson and H. R. Luard added, half green morocco, uncut, top edges gilt* 6 vol.
₊ Mr. Luard was the principal compiler and editor of this Catalogue and on the fly-leaves he has added the sums paid to the various Cataloguers. He has also added manuscript notes on margins.

166 Cambridge Essays for 1855, 1856 and 1858, 3 vol. 1855-58 —Sandars (S.) Great St. Mary's Church, *Cambridge,* 1869—Boyce (E. J.) Memorial of the Cambridge Camden Society, 1888—Cambridge Antiquarian Society's Octavo Publication, No. 5 and No. 8 to 10, 12 to 24, and 26—Ecclesiologist, No. 106—Reports of Cambridge Antiquarian Society from 1842 to 1891 inclusive ; Lists of Members, &c. &c. *a bundle*

167 Cambridge. Statutes of Trinity College, 1882-89— Emmanuel College Tercentenary Festival, *portrait of Founder,* 1884—Admissions to St. John the Evangelist College, 16$\frac{44}{30}$-1665, 1882 ; and 3 others relating to Cambridge (6)

168 Cambridge University Calendar for 1890, *Camb.* 1890— The same for 1812, *ib.* 1812—Warwick (W. A.) Cambridge University Register, *ib.* 1844—Spalding (W. P.) Cambridge Directory for 1884 and 1887, 2 vol. *plan, ib.* 1884-87— Railway Traveller's Walk through Cambridge, *ib.* 1880 (6)

169 Cambridge University Pamphlets, viz. The light Green, 2 Nos. *Camb.* 1872—Birks (T. R.) Inaugural Lecture, 1872—Cope (E. M.) Review of Aristotle's Ethics, 1867 ; and other Tracts (1872-90) in the Volume, *half calf gilt*

170 Cambridge University Tracts by Peacock, Perry, Hopkins, Kennedy, Frend, Marriott, Williams, Christian, Bp. Monk, &c. &c. in 4 vol. *half calf gilt* *v. y.*

170*Cambridge University. A Collection of over 100 Tracts relating to the University, published between 1740 and 1868, bound in 5 vol. *half calf*

171 Cambridgeshire and Isle of Ely Churches by the Cambridge Camden Society, *plates, half Roxburghe, uncut, Cambridge,* 1845—Cambridgeshire by E. W. Brayley and J. Britton, LARGE PAPER, *map and plates (from Beauties of England), half morocco, uncut, top edge gilt,* 1809 (2)

172 Campbell (J. Lord) Lives of the Lord Chancellors and Keepers of the Great Seal of England, 8 vol. *calf extra* 1846 69

173 Cantabrigienses Graduati (1669-1823), *half calf gilt,*
Cantab. 1823—Musæ Cantabrigienses, *half calf,* 1810 (2)
174 Cautley (G. S.) Century of Emblems, *woodcut illustra-*
tions, ornamented cloth, gilt edges   1878
175 Carlyle (T.) Chartism, 1858—Wynter (A.) Curiosities of
Civilization, 1860—Senior (N. W.) Political Economy,
1850—Brimley (G.) Essays, *portrait, Camb.* 1858 (4)
176 Carmina Ethica ex diversis Auctoribus collegit A. A.
Renouard, LARGE PAPER, *russia, by Roger Payne, with*
Wodhull arms in gold on sides   *Paris.* 1795
177 Carmen Sylva (Elisabetta di Romania) Novelle, *Milano,*
1888—Boccacci (G.) Decameron, *ib.* 1875—Verga (G.)
Novelle e Novelle Rusticane, 2 vol. *ib.* 1880-83—
Gherardi del Testa (T.) La Povera e la Ricca, *Firenze,*
1858 ; and 7 others, Italian   (12)
178 Carter (E.) History of Cambridge University, *old panelled*
calf   1721
179 Carter (E.) History of the County of Cambridge, LARGE
PAPER *(only* 40 *copies printed), tree-marbled calf extra,*
uncut, top edge gilt   1819
180 Cartier (E.) Life of Beato Angelico da Fiesole, *frontis-*
piece and head pieces   1865
181 Cassan (S. H.) Lives of the Bishops of Sherborne and
Salisbury, *Salisbury,* 1824—Lives of the Bishops of
Winchester, 2 vol. *Frome,* 1827—Lives of the Bishops of
Bath and Wells, *ib.* 1829, *ports. and plates, calf extra*
4 *vol.*
182 Catalogue of the Portsmouth Collection of Books and
Papers written by or belonging to Sir Isaac Newton,
drawn up by the Syndicate (H. R. Luard, G. G. Stokes,
J. C. Adams and G. D. Liveing), LARGE PAPER *(only*
a few copies printed, see J. Porter's autograph letter
added), red morocco extra, uncut, t. e. g. Cambridge, 1888
183 Catonis (D.) Disticha de Moribus Gr. et Lat. cum Notis
Variorum et O. Arntzenii, *frontispiece, half gilt calf,*
uncut   *Amst.* 1754
184 CATULLUS, TIBULLUS, PROPETIUS (*sic*) *with corrected*
title at end, old calf   *Venetiis, Aldus,* 1502
  ₊ Very scarce. Mr. Beckford's copy sold for £16, and
Sir J. Thorold's for £9 15s.
185 Cazenove (J. G.) on the Being and Attributes of God,
1886—Salmon (G.) Trinity College Chapel, Dublin,
Sermons, *Camb.* 1861—Myers (T.) Conciones Basilicæ
on Second Advent, 1844—Westcott (B. F.) From
Strength to Strength, 1890—Baring-Gould (S.) Post
Mediæval Preachers, 1865—Sermons during Holy
Week in the Chapel of Culham Training College, *Ox-*
ford, 1860   (6)

186 Cellini (B.) Vita, *half vellum, Milano,* 1874—D'Azeglio
(M.) I miei Ricordi, *half calf extra, Firenze,* 1881—Re
(Z.) Vita di Cola di Rienzo, *half bound, ib.* 1854 (3)

187 Cervantes Saavedra (M. de) Don Quixote, translated by
C. Jarvis, 4 vol. *coloured plates, calf gilt* 1819

188 Cervantes (M. de) Don Quixote, translated by T. Smollett, 3 vol. *illustrations by G. Cruikshank* 1833

189 Chalmers (A.) Notes and Life of Shakspeare, *portraits,*
half calf gilt *Paris,* 1839

190 Chatterton (T.) Poems of T. Rowley and others, with
Vindication of the Appendix, by T. Tyrwhitt, 2 vol.
in 1, *half morocco* 1778-82

191 Chatterton (T.) Poetical Works, 2 vol. 1871

192 Children's Books, by Mrs. Trimmer, Berquin, &c. *with*
plates *a parcel*

193 Christa Sangita, History of Christ, in Sanscrit Verse,
with English Introduction, by Mill, 5 vol. in 1, *half red*
morocco *Calcutta,* 1834-42

194 Christmas Garland of Carols and Poems, edited by A. H.
Bullen, LARGE PAPER, 7 *illustrations by H. G. Wells on*
Japanese paper 1885

195 Chronicles of the White Rose of York, a Series of Historical
Fragments, with Notes, &c. (by James Bohn) *portrait*
of Edward IV and plate, half Roxburghe, uncut 1845

196 Chronicon Angliæ Petriburgense, edidit J. A. Giles, 1845

197 Church and World : Essays, by various Writers, edited by
Rev. O. Shipley 1866

198 Church Pamphlets. James on the Rubric, Church Ornaments and Ministers, 1866 ; and 27 other Tracts on the
subject in the volume, *half calf gilt* 1866-71

199 Church Psalter and Hymn Book, by W. Mercer and J.
Goss, *with music,* 1856—Hymns, edited by W. H.
Monk, *with music, n. d.*—Hymns and Verses, by G. T.
1866—Palmer (R.) Book of Praise, 1863—Sacred
Poetry, Second Series, *Edinb. n. d.* (5)

200 Church Quarterly Review, from October 1875 to January
1891, 31 vol. *half calf gilt* 1876-91

201 Churton (E.) Poetical Remains, *red morocco extra, gilt*
edges 1876

202 Ciceronis Epistolæ ad Atticum, Brutum et Quintum
Fratrem *Venetiis, Aldus,* 1548

203 Ciceronis Epistolæ Familiares, *old olive morocco lined with*
red leather, gilt edges, by Desseuil *Lutetiæ,* 1578

204 Ciceronis Opera cum Clavi J. A. Ernesti, 12 vol. *Regent's*
Edition, uncut 1820

205 Clarendon (E. Earl of) History of the Rebellion, with the
suppressed Passages, 7 vol. *Oxford,* 1849—Life and
Continuation of the History, 2 vol. *ib.* 1857 9 *vol.*

206 Claretie (J.) Le troisième dessous, *Paris*, 1882—Racine (J.) Œuvres, *half calf extra, ib.* 1840—Dickens (C.) Nicolas Nickleby traduit par P. Lorain, 2 vol. *ib. s. d.*— Girardin (Madame E. de) Le Marquis de Pontanges, *ib.* 1861—Madlle. de Launay à la Bastille, *ib.* 1813 (6)

207 Clark (H.) Introduction to Heraldry, *plates*   1873

208 Clark (W. G.) Peloponnesus, *map and plans, presentation copy, with author's autograph inscription and letter in Greek, and also with an autograph letter from H. A. J. Munro describing Clark's funeral and giving Cambridge Gossip*   1858

209 Clarke (E. D.) Life and Remains, by Bp. W. Otter, 2 vol. *portrait, calf gilt*   1825

210 Clarke (W.) Repertorium Bibliographicum, 2 vol. LARGE PAPER, *india proof portraits and plates, tree marbled calf extra, uncut, by Zaehnsdorf*   1819

211 Classical Journal, from 1810 to 1829 inclusive, 80 Nos. in 40 vol.   1810-29

212 Classical Museum, 7 vol. *calf extra*   1844-50

213 Classical Pamphlets, in 4 vol. *half calf gilt*   (45)

214 Classical Review, 40 Nos. in 4 vol. *cloth;* and vol. V, No. 1 to 4, *unbound*   1887-91

215 Clay (W. K.) Histories of Waterbeach, Landbeach, Horningsea and Milton, 4 vol. in 1, *plates, half red morocco, uncut, top edge gilt*   *Cambridge,* 1859-61-65-69

216 Coleridge (Rt. Hon. Sir J. T.) Memoir of Rev. J. Keble   *Oxford,* 1870

217 Coleridge (S. T.) Aids to Reflection, *morocco, g. e.*   1867

218 Coleridge (S. T.) Poetical and Dramatic Works, 3 vol. *W. Pickering,* 1844—The Friend, 3 vol. *ib.* 1844— Church and State, and Lay Sermons, *ib.* 1839   7 *vol.*

219 Collection of British Authors, Tauchnitz Edition   25 *vol.*

220 Colonna (F.) Strife of Love, in a Dream, being the Elizabethan Version, edited by A. Lang, *woodcuts*   1890

221 Comicorum Græcorum Fragmenta cum Historia critica, edidit A. Meineke, 4 vol. in 5, *calf gilt*   *Berolini,* 1839-41

222 Comicorum Græcorum Fragmenta cum Versionibus Latinis et Anglicis, edidit J. Bailey, *half russia, with autograph letter of the author added, Cantab.* 1840— Comicorum Græcorum Fragmenta, Gr. Lat. et Anglice cum Notis R. Walpole, *ib.* 1805   (2)

223 Comines (P. de) Memoires avec Supplement, 4 vol. *portraits, old calf*   *Brusselle,* 1706-13

224 Constable's Miscellany, 49 vol.   *Edinb.* 1826-33

225 Conway (W. M.) Woodcutters of the Netherlands in the XVth Century, *autograph letter of H. Bradshaw added*
Cambridge, 1884

226 Cooper (C. H.) and T. Cooper, Athenæ Cantabrigienses (1500-1609), 2 vol. *with autograph letter of Cooper, and " In Memoriam " by J. E. B. Mayor added*
Camb. 1858-61

227 Cooper (C. H.) Memoir of Margaret, Countess of Richmond and Derby, *portrait, autograph inscription of J. E. Mayor, the editor* *ib.* 1874

228 Cowper (W.) Poetical Works, 3 vol. *portrait, red morocco extra, gilt edges* *W. Pickering,* 1843

229 Cope (E. M.) Introduction to Aristotle's Rhetoric, *author's autograph letter added, Cambridge,* 1867— Aristotelis Rhetorica, Gr. et Lat. cum Notis Variorum, 2 vol. *half russia, Oxonii,* 1820 *3 vol.*

230 Coplestone (Bp. E.) Advice to a Young Reviewer, and Three Replies to Edinburgh Review to its Calumnies against Oxford, in 1 vol. *half calf gilt, Oxford,* 1807-11

231 Cornhill Magazine, from January 1860 to June 1883 inclusive, 47 vol. *plates, half calf gilt* 1860-83

232 Costantino Canonico Castellano, *Torino,* 1870 ; and other Poems by the same in the volume, *half bound ; from the Library of Monsignor Anivitti*

233 Councils and Ecclesiastical Documents relating to Great Britain and Ireland, edited after Spelman and Wilkins by A. W. Haddan and W. Stubbs, 3 vol. *uncut*
Oxford, 1869-78

234 Cox (G. V.) Recollections of Oxford, 1868—Oxford Ten Year Book, completed to 1870, *Oxford,* 1872—Companion to the Guide and Guide to the Companion, *ib.* 1800 (3)

235 Crabb (J.) Gipsies' Advocate, 1831—Plutarch's Life of Themistocles, in Greek, with Notes by H. A. Holden, 1881—Stuart (J.) and N. Revett, Antiquities of Athens, *plates,* 1837—Bartlett (W. H.) Pilgrimage through the Holy Land, *plates, half calf gilt* (1854)—Neale (J. M.) Notes on Dalmatia, Croatia, Istria, Styria, and Visit to Montenegro, *plates,* 1861—Howells (W. D.) Venetian Life, vol. I, *Edinb.* 1883—Three Weeks in Palestine and Lebanon, *plates,* 1833 (7)

236 Crabbe (G.) Works, 5 vol. *tree-marbled calf extra* 1823

237 Craven née La Ferronnays (Madame Augustus) Récit d'une Sœur : Souvenir de Famille, 2 vol. *half bound*
Paris, 1868

238 Craven (Madame Augustus) Une Année de Méditations
ib. 1881

QUARTO.

239 ACADEMY (THE), a Monthly Record of Literature, Learning, Science and Art, from 9 October 1869 to December 1890 inclusive, 38 vol. (*vol. I to XV half calf gilt, and the rest in cloth*), and from January to 4 April, 1891, 14 Nos. *unbound* 1869-91

240 Æliani Variæ Historiæ : Ex Heraclide de Rebus publicis Commentarium ; Polemonis et Adamantis Physionomia ; Melampodis ex Palpitationibus Divinatio ; et de Nevis. Omnia Græce, FIRST EDITION, *fine copy in vellum*
Romæ, 1545

241 Æschyli Tragœdiæ cum Scholiis, Græce Cura P. Victorii, *fine copy in blue morocco* *H. Stephanus*, 1557

242 Æschyli Tragœdia Septem-Thebana, Gr. et Lat. Q. Septimio Florente Christiano Interprete, 2 vol. in 1, *fine copy in russia, gilt edges* *Lutetiæ*, 1585

243 Æschylus Eumenides, in Greek and English, as arranged for Performance, *with the incidental music by C. V. Stanford, 5 programmes added, Cambridge*, 1885—Catalogue of Editions of Æschylus in the British Museum, 1883 (2)

244 Agostino da Montefeltro (Padre) Quaresimale, *portrait*
Roma, 1889

245 Anstey (C.) Poetical Works, with his Life by his Son, *portrait and plates, calf extra, gilt edges* 1808

246 ANTHOLOGIA GRÆCA Literis Capitalibus (Cura J. Lascaris), FIRST EDITION, *with the genuine Latin letter of Lascaris rigidly suppressed when Peter de' Medicis, to whom it is addressed, fled from Florence a proscribed man, morocco extra, gilt edges* *Florentiæ per L. de Alopa*, 1494
* Extremely rare. Askew's copy sold for £15 15s.

247 Anthologia Græca, *MS. notes by Claud Groulart (chiefly translations by Alciati, Politian, &c.), old calf*
H. Stephanus, 1566

248 APOLLONII RHODII ARGONAUTICA, cum Scholiis, Græce, FIRST EDITION, *Text printed in capital letters, autograph of* " Theodorus Phearus Petroburgus," *fine copy in old English red morocco, gilt edges*
(Florentiæ, F. de Alopa), 1496
* Extremely rare. Didot's copy sold for 364 francs, and Sir J. Thorold's for £17 15s.

249 Apollonii Rhodii Argonautica cum Scholiis, Græce, et cum Notis H. Stephani, *autographs of J. Tunstall, J. Taylor and G. Burges, old russia* *H. Stephanus*, 1574

250 Aristæneti Epistolæ Eroticæ, Græce, FIRST EDITION, *ruled*
Antverpiæ, C. Plantinus, 1566

251 Aristoteles de Poetica, Gr. et Lat. cum Notis T. Tyrwhitt, LARGE PAPER, *portrait of Tyrwhitt added, old gilt calf extra* Oxonii, 1794

252 Aristophanes' Peace and Wasps, in Greek and English, with Notes by B. B. Rogers, 2 vol. 1866-75

253 Bartolozzi (F.) and his Works, by A. W. Tuer, 2 vol. *plates, vellum, uncut* 1881

254 Batten (E. C.) Life of Bp. R. Fox and his Register (1292-94), *autograph letter of author added* 1889

255 Beaconsfield (B. Disraeli, Earl of) Cartoons from Punch, 105 *illustrations* 1878

256 Bentham (J.) History of Ely Cathedral, with Supplement by W. Stevenson, 2 vol. *portrait and plates, uncut* Norwich, 1812-17

257 Bentleii (R.) et Doctorum Virorum Epistolæ partim mutuæ. Accedit R. Dawesii ad J. Taylorum Epistola, LARGE PAPER, *open letter proof portraits of Bentley and Grævius, half calf extra, back broken* 1807

*** Only 100 copies printed by Dr. Burney for presents.

258 Bentley. Horatius cum Notis R. Bentleii, LARGE PAPER, *frontispiece, old calf* Amst. 1713

259 Bentley. Lucani Pharsalia cum Notis H. Grotii et R. Bentleii, edente R. Cumberland, *old calf* Strawberry Hill, 1760

260 Bentley. Manilii Astronomicon cum Notis R. Bentleii, LARGE PAPER, *portrait of Bentley by Vertue, and plates, old calf* 1739

*** Scarce on Large Paper. Dent's sold for £5 18s.

261 Bentley. Middleton (C.) Remarks on Bentley's Proposals for Greek Testament, 1721 — Bentley's Proposals, 1721 —Middleton (C.) Farther Remarks upon the Proposals, 1721—Letter to Bentley, 1721 — Pearce (Z.) Epistolæ duæ, 1721 — Colbach (J.) Jus Academicum, 1722; *half calf gilt in 1 vol.*

262 Bentley. Milton (J.) Paradise Lost: a new Edition by R. Bentley, 2 *portraits by Vertue, autograph of Wm. Cowper (the Poet), and numerous holograph notes of W. Hayley, tree-marbled calf extra by Wilson* 1732

263 Bentley (R.) Plautine Emendations by E. A. Sonnenschein Oxford, 1883

264 Bentley. Terentii Comœdiæ cum Notis G. Faerni et R. Bentleii. Accedunt Phædri Fabulæ, P. Syri et aliorum Veterum Sententiæ, LARGE PAPER, *plates, old calf* Amst. 1727

265 Bersezio (V.) Roma, la Capitale d'Italia, *numerous illustrations, half calf gilt* Roma, s. a.

266 Bible (Cambridge Paragraph) by Rev. F. H. Scrivener, 3 vol. *Cambridge,* 1870-73

267 Bibliographer (The) a Journal of Book-Lore, from December 1881 to November 1884 inclusive, 6 vol. 1881-84— Book-Lore, a Magazine devoted to Old Time Literature, from December 1884 to November 1887 inclusive, 6 vol. 1884-87, *half morocco* 12 *vol.*

268 Bibliotheca Literaria, 10 Nos. in 1 vol. *half bound, uncut* 1722-24

269 Bion et Moschus, Græce edente G. Wakefield, LARGE PAPER, *half russia, uncut, top edge gilt* 1795

270 Blakhal (G.) Narration of the Services done to three noble Ladyes (Madame de Gordon, Ladye Isabelle Hay and Sophia Countess of Aboyne), 1631-49, *calf extra, gilt edges* *Aberdeen for Spalding Club,* 1844

271 Blomefield (F.) Collectanea Cantabrigiensia, *old calf* *Norwich,* 1750

272 Blomfield (Bp. C. J.) Speech on the Roman Catholic Relief Bill, 27 May, 1828—AUTOGRAPH MS. *with 2 holograph letters and 2 Franks of the Bishop added, half morocco* 1828-31

273 Book of Deer, edited for the Spalding Club by J. Stuart, *plates, including facsimiles* *Edinb.* 1869

⁎ Contains the Gospels and Creed in Latin.

274 Brookes (S.) Introduction to the Study of Conchology, *coloured plates* 1815

275 Bruce (J. C.) Bayeux Tapestry elucidated, *coloured plates* 1856

276 Butler (Bp. S.) Atlas of ancient and modern Geography, 23 *coloured maps* *n. d.*

277 Byrom (J.) Library Catalogue, *view of his house and photograph portraits, calf gilt* 1848

⁎ A few copies printed for private circulation only.

278 Byrom (J.) Private Journal and Literary Remains, edited by R. Parkinson, 4 parts in 2 vol. *portrait and pedigrees, calf, gilt* *Printed for the Chetham Society,* 1854-57

279 Cambridge (R. O.) Works, with Life by his Son, *portraits and plates, russia extra* 1803

280 Cambridge Antiquarian Society's Publications, vol. I, *plates (several coloured), half red morocco, top edge gilt ;* and No. 13, 14 and 15 *with 18 plates, unbound* *Cambridge,* 1846-49

281 Cambridge Camden Society's Transactions, *half calf gilt* *ib.* 1841

282 Cambridge. Statuta Collegii S. Trinitatis, *green morocco extra, gilt edges, with Trinity College Arms in gold on sides* *Cantab.* 1844

283 Cambridge. The Tatler, in Cambridge May Term, 1871, and Lent Term, 1872, 2 vol. *half calf gilt, Camb.* 1871-72

284 CAMDEN SOCIETY'S PUBLICATIONS. FIRST SERIES, with descriptive Catalogue of J. G. Nichols and Index, 107 *volumes, a complete set, uncut, with the exception of* " Promptorium Parvulorum," *vol.* 25, 54 *and* 89, *which have been bound by Zaehnsdorf, in orange morocco extra, borders of gold, gilt edges, and wanting No.* 95 *Manipulus Vocabulorum,* 105 vol. in 102, 1838-81—NEW SERIES, 49 volumes, all published, *uncut,* 1871-91
(152 *vol.*)

285 Cartularium Saxonicum : a collection of Charters relating to Anglo-Saxon History, by W. de Gray Birch, 27 Parts   1883-90

286 Cary (J.) English Atlas, *set of County maps, half russia*
1787

287 Catalano da S. Mauro (N.) Fiume del Terrestre Paradiso. Discorso sopra l'antica Forma dell' Habito Minoritico da S. Francesco d'Assisi, *plates, vellum*   *Fiorenza,* 1652

288 Catalogue of Charterhouse School Library, with the Addenda, *autograph letter of A. H. Tod added, and MS. additions*   *Godalming,* 1882-84

289 Catullus. Recensuit J. Wilkes, *red morocco, gilt edges,* 1788

  ₄ Wilkes, for a wager to print a work without an error, issued this edition, of which only a few copies were printed for presents. Sir J. Thorold's copy sold for £2 14s.

290 Cellini (B.) Life, translated by J. A. Symonds, 2 vol. *portrait and 8 etchings by F. Laguillermie, half Roxburghe, uncut, top edges gilt*   1888

291 Challoner (R.) Britannia Sancta, or Lives of British, English, Scottish and Irish Saints, 2 vol. in 1, *russia extra, leather joints, gilt edges*   1745

292 Charitonis Aphrodisiensis Amatoriæ Narrationes de Chærea et Callirrhoe Gr. et Lat. cum Notis J. P. D'Orville, 2 vol. *red morocco extra, gilt edges*   *Amst.* 1750

293 Chaucer (G.) Canterbury Tales with Essay, Notes and Glossary by T. Tyrwhitt, 2 vol. *portrait of Tyrwhitt, morocco extra, gilt edges*   *Oxford,* 1798

294 Chaucer (G.) The Clerk's Tale, printed from MS. in Cambridge University Library   1867

295 Chronicles of the Ancient British Church previous to the Arrival of St. Augustine   1851

296 Chronicon de Lanercost (1201-1346) edidit J. Stevenson, *half russia*   *Edinb.* 1839

  ₄ Presented to the Bannatyne Club by W. Macdowall.

297 Ciceronis Rhetorica ad Herennium et alia Opera Rhetorica,
 vellum *Venetiis, Aldus,* 1521
298 Clarke (E. D.) Tomb of Alexander, *plates, Cambridge,* 1805
299 Dalechamp (C.) Christian Hospitalitie handled common-
 place-wise in the Chappel of Trinity Colledge in Cambridge.
 Wherunto is added Life and Death of Mr. Harrison, the
 late Hospital Vice-Master of that Societie, *vellum*
 Cambridge, 1632
 *** Very scarce, unknown to Lowndes.
300 Dante Alighieri Comedia con la nova Espositione di A.
 Vellutello, *woodcuts, half russia*
 Vinegia, F. Marcolini, 1544
 *** First Edition, with the Commentary of Vellutello, and
 very scarce. Roscoe's copy sold for £4 14s. 6d.
301 Dibdin (T. F.) Typographical Antiquities, 4 vol. *portraits
 and facsimiles, with List of early English Printers and
 Books, added, calf extra* 1810-19

FOLIO.

302 Æschyli Tragœdiæ, Græce, LARGE PAPER, *illustrated with
 Flaxman's designs, calf gilt* *Glasguæ, A. Foulis,* 1795
 *** Sir M. Sykes's copy with Flaxman's illustrations sold
 for £14 10s.
303 Æschyli Tragœdiæ. Another copy, *without Flaxman's
 designs, half calf, uncut* *ib.* 1795
304 Ammiani Marcellini Res gestæ cura Jacobi Gronovii,
 LARGE PAPER, *plates, old calf* *Lugd. Bat.* 1693
305 Anglicanæ Historiæ Scriptores varii nunc primum editi a
 J. Sparke, LARGEST PAPER (*only* 25 *copies printed*),
 calf gilt 1723
306 ANGLICARUM RERUM SCRIPTORES VETERES, edentibus J.
 Fell et T. Gale, 3 vol. *fine copy in red morocco extra,
 borders of gold, gilt edges, by Mackenzie*
 Oxoniæ, 1684-91-87
307 Antonelli (Cardinale L.) Memorie storiche delle sacre
 Teste dei Santi Apostoli Petro e Paolo e della loro
 solenne Ricognizione nella Basilica Lateranense, *plates,
 half vellum* *Roma,* 1852
308 Appiani Romanæ Historiæ, Græce, FIRST EDITION,
 Lutetiæ, C. Stephanus, 1551—Appiani Historiæ Latine,
 P. Candido Interprete, *with autograph and motto of Lord
 Poyntz, Paris.* 1538, *old calf extra* *in* 1 *vol.*
309 ARISTOPHANIS COMŒDIÆ NOVEM, cum Scholiis, Græce
 Cura M. Musuri, FIRST EDITION, *fine copy in russia
 extra, gilt edges* *Venetiis, Aldus,* 1498
 *** Very rare. Sir J. Thorold's copy sold for £13.

310 Arnobii Disputationes adversus Gentes et Minucii Felicis Octavius (*printed as Book VIII of Arnobius*), FIRST EDITION, *MS. Note of Rev. S. Martin, vellum, Romæ,* 1542 *⁎*⁎* Rare. Sir J. Thorold's copy sold for £2 4s.

311 Art de verifier les Dates, 3 vol. *fine copy in old gilt veau marbré* *Paris,* 1783-87

312 Arundel Society, *five large heads engraved in outline ;* and sundry Prospectuses of the Society *a parcel*

313 Athenæus Græce Cura M. Musuri, FIRST EDITION, *old calf, slightly wormed, sold with all faults, Venetiis, Aldus,* 1514
⁎⁎* Scarce. The Wodhull copy sold for £6 10s. On title is written "Ambrosius Ypphofer Custos et Canonicus Brixinenensis emit Venetiis duobus aureis, uno et dimidiato 1518."

314 Augustini (Beati) Liber qui vocatur Quinquaginta (Homiliæ), *fine copy in red morocco, gilt edges* *Augustæ, A. Sorg,* 1475

315 AULI GELII NOCTES ATTICÆ, *bordered initial letter illuminated in gold and colours, slightly stained, brown morocco extra, gilt edges*
Venetiis, per Andream Jacobi Catherensem, 1477
⁎⁎* Scarce. Sir J. Thorold's copy sold for £8 5s.

316 Balei (J.) Scriptorum illustrium Majoris Britanniæ XIV Centuriæ, 2 vol. in 1, *portrait, slightly wormed, calf extra, gilt edges, sold with all faults* *Basileæ,* 1557-59

317 Bartholomei [degli Albizzi] de Pisis Opus intitulatum de Conformitate Vitæ B. Francisci ad Vitam Domini Jesu Christi, *with 22 coloured engravings by Picart, illustrating the life of St. Francis inserted at end. fine copy in red morocco extra, broad dentelle borders of gold, silk linings, gilt edges, by Derome* *Mediolani,* 1513

318 Bayeux Tapestry, 17 *coloured plates, scarce* 1819-23

319 BENTLEY. LUCRETIUS DE RERUM NATURA, cum Commentariis perpetuis, Animadversionibus R. BENTLEII non ante vulgatis et Notis Variorum curante G. Wakefield, 3 vol. LARGE PAPER, *proof portrait of Wakefield added, fine copy in gilt russia, by Roger Payne, with Wodhull arms in gold on sides* 1796-97
⁎⁎* Extremely rare, most of the large paper copies having been destroyed in the fire at the printers. Edwards's copy sold for £55 13s., and Heathcote's for £52 10s.

320 Bentley. T. Bishop of Ely *v.* R. Bentley, Bentley's case, *with K. B. Judgment endorsed in MS.*—Case of Bp. of Ely—Appendix to Bentley's Case, *very rare* *n. d.*

321 Bergomensis (Jacobi Philippi Foresti) Chronicarum Supplementum, *woodcuts, oak boards covered in parchment, with clasps* *Venetiis,* 1486

322 Bickersteth (E. H.) Commentary on the New Testament (with the Text), *portrait of Bickersteth, presentation copy with author's autograph inscription* 1864

323 Bingham (J.) Works, 2 vol. *old panelled calf, backs broken* 1726

324 Block Book. Biblia Pauperum, reproduced in facsimile with Introduction by J. P. Berjeau, *cuts illustrating the Bible, half bound, uncut* 1859

325 Bradshaw (Henry) Half Century of Notes on the Day-Book of John Dorne, Bookseller in Oxford, A.D. 1520, as edited by F. Madan for the Oxford Historical Society, MANUSCRIPT *Cambridge*, 1886

326 Brown (E.) Fasciculus Rerum expetendarum et fugiendarum, 2 vol. 1690

327 CÆSARIS QUÆ EXTANT, cum Notis S. Clarke, *portrait of the Duke of Marlborough, and 85 large engravings (including the famous Buffalo), in perfect condition, green morocco extra, gilt edges* 1712

328 Cambridge Examination Papers (1834 to 1857), in 4 vol. *half calf;* and various others from 1847 to 1870, loose in a portfolio (5)

329 Cambridge. Trinity College and University Papers and Documents, collected by Dr. Luard and bound in 1 vol. *half morocco* 1846-59

330 Cambridge University Report, *half calf gilt* 1852

331 Cambridgeshire Domesday Book, *photo-zincographed facsimile*, 1862—Walker (B.) Tabular Analysis of Cambridgeshire Domesday *Camb.* 1884

332 Castiglione (Conte B.) Il Cortegiano, FIRST EDITION, *in old Venetian stamped calf, with figure of a boy carrying a sail in gold on sides* *Venetia, Aldo*, 1528

*** A scarce edition, the one cited by the Academy of Crusca. Wodhull's copy sold for £3 3s.

333 CHRONICON NUREMBERGENSE (Auctore H. Schedel) large copy (18½ by 12¾ inches), *very slightly wormed and folio CXLVII to CLII damaged but mended, upwards of 2250 spirited woodcuts (many very large and including 2 very curious views of London) by M. Wolgemut (Master of Albert Durer) and W. Pleydenwurff, vellum, sold with all faults* *Nurembergæ, A. Koberger*, 1493

334 Ciaconii (A.) Vita et Res gestæ Pontificum Romanorum et Cardinalium, 2 vol. *portraits and coats of arms, vellum* *Romæ*, 1630

335 Ciceronis Tusculanæ Quæstiones, *vellum* *Venetiis, N. Jenson*, 1472

*** Very scarce. Edwards's copy sold for £7 7s. and was resold in Wodhull's for £6.

336 Columbus (C.) Secret Logboke, Facsimile of a forged Manuscript with Drawings including Map of Hayti, *in a case*
E. Stock, 1890
337 Craffonara (G.) I più celebri Quadri delle diverse Scuole
Italiane riuniti nell' Appartamento Borgia del Vaticano
descritti da G. A. Guattani, 41 *plates, calf extra, gilt
edges, with crest of Earl of Clare in gold on sides*
Roma, 1820
338 Dante Alighieri L'Inferno, il Purgatorio ed il Paradiso,
3 vol. in 2, *illustrations by G. Doré, half red morocco,
uncut* *Parigi*, 1861-68
339 Dionysii Halicarnassei Antiquitates Romanæ Græce, FIRST
EDITION, *Lutetiæ, R. Stephanus,* 1546-47—Idem de
Compositione Orationis, de Arte Rhetorica et de quo
Genere dicendi sit Usus Thucydides, Græce, *ib.* 1547
in 1 *vol.*

SECOND DAY'S SALE.

OCTAVO ET INFRA.

LOT
340 Crawford (Earl of) Hand-List of early Editions of Greek
and Latin Writers and of a few of the rarer Vocabula-
ries and Grammars, *autograph letter of Earl of Crawford added* 1885
*** Only 50 copies printed for presents.
341 Cripps (W. J.) Old English Plate, its Makers and Marks,
Second Edition, 73 *illustrations* 1881
342 Croft (Sir H.) Love and Madness in a Series of Letters
(*Correspondence of the beautiful Miss Margaret Reay,
Mistress of Earl of Sandwich, and Rev. Mr. Hackman
hung for her murder*) *portrait of Earl of Sandwich added,
tree-marbled calf extra, uncut* 1780
343 Croker (T. C.) Fairy Legends and Traditions of the South
of Ireland, *woodcuts* 1863
344 Crowe (J. A.) and G. B. Cavalcaselle, New History of
Painting in Italy, 3 vol. *plates, cloth* 1864-66
345 Crowe (J. A.) and G. B. Cavalcaselle, Titian his Life and
Times, 2 vol. *portrait and illustrations, cloth, uncut,* 1877
346 Crowe (J. A.) and G. B. Cavalcaselle, Raphael, his Life
and Works, 2 vol. *cloth* 1882-85

347 Cruden (A.) Concordance to the Old and New Testament
and to the Apocrypha, *portrait* 1836

348 CRUIKSHANK. Brough (R. B.) Life of Sir John Falstaff,
plates by Geo. Cruikshank, half gilt morocco, m. e.
roy. 8vo. 1858

349 Cruikshank (G.) Forty Illustrations of Lord Byron, *in the*
original cover *n. d.*

350 Cumberland (R.) Memoirs by Himself, 2 vol. *portraits,*
calf gilt, 1807—Mudford (W.) Critical Examination of
the Writings of R. Cumberland, 2 vol. *portrait, calf*
gilt, 1812 *4 vol.*

351 Cunningham (W.) Churches of Asia, *frontispiece,* 1880—
Todd (J. H.) Books of the Vaudois, *Dublin,* 1865—
Cambridge Lent Sermons, edited by H. R. Luard, *Camb.*
1864—Spiritual Letters of S. Francis de Sales, 1871—
Sewell (Elizabeth M.) Passing Thoughts on Religion,
1860—Thomas a Kempis of the Imitation of Christ,
Oxford, 1841 (6)

352 Cunningham (W.) Dissertation on the Epistle of St. Bar-
nabas, 1877—Aitken (R.) High Truth, 1866—Westcott
(B. F.) Gospel of the Resurrection, *Camb.* 1867—Smith
(W. S.) Blood of the Covenant, *ib.* 1889—Churton
(W. R.) Influence of the Septuagint on Christianity, *ib.*
1861—Shairp (J. C.) Culture and Religion, *Edinb.*
1871 (6)

353 Cunningham (W.) Hulsean Lectures on St. Austin, 1886
—Christian Opinion of Usury, *frontispiece,* 1884 (2)

354 Curci (C. M.) Il Moderno Dissidio tra la Chiesa e l'Italia,
Firenze, 1878—La Nuova Italia ed i Vecchi Zelanti, *ib.*
1881 *2 vol.*

355 Cyrilli Patriarchæ Alexandrini (Sancti) Commentarius
in S. Lucæ Evangelium cum aliorum aliquot Patrum
Fragmentis Græce Cura Angelli Maii Cardinalis S.
Anastasiæ, THICK PAPER, *red calf extra, borders of gold,*
gilt edges, very scarce *Romæ,* 1838

356 Dante Alighieri Opere Poetiche, 2 vol. *portrait, half calf*
extra *Parigi,* 1836

357 Dante's Inferno in literal Prose, by J. A. Carlyle, *portrait,*
1889—Purgatory and Paradise in Italian and English,
by A. J. Butler, 2 vol. 1880-85—Dante, an Essay by
R. W. Church, with Translation "de Monarchia," by
F. J. Church, 1878 (4)

358 Darling (C. J.) Scintillæ Juris, LARGE PAPER (*one of* 75
copies), *frontispiece* 1889

359 Davis (W.) Olio, *half red morocco, gilt edges* 1817

360 Day (M.) Catalogue of printed Books in Worcester
Cathedral Library *Oxford,* 1880

361 Dawes (R.) Extracts from a MS. Pamphlet, *intitled* "Tittle-Tattle Mongers," *half red morocco*
Newcastle-upon-Tyne, 1747

*** On the fly-leaf, Mr. Crossley has a long note concerning the excessive rarity of this Tract, commencing "There are few rarer Tracts in the English Language." Trotter Brockett's imperfect copy sold for £4 5s., and Mr. Dyce, in his Life of Akenside, styles this Pamphlet " so scarce that I have never been able to procure a sight of it."

362 Dawesii (R.) Miscellanea Critica cum Notis T. Kidd, *autograph letter of Kidd added, Cantab.* 1817—Horatii Opera edidit T. Kidd, LARGE PAPER, *ib.* 1817—Opuscula Ruhnkeniana, edidit T. Kidd, 1807, *vellum extra, 3 vol.*

363 Decretales Pseudo-Isidorianæ et Capitula Angilramni cum Commentatione P. Hinschii, *tree-marbled extra*
Lipsiæ, 1863

364 Delepierre (O.) Macaroneana, *uncut*   *Paris.* 1852

365 Dennis (G.) Cities and Cemeteries of Etruria, 2 vol. *map, plans and illustrations, half red morocco extra, uncut, top edges gilt*   1878

366 Description of 300 Animals, *numerous woodcuts*, 1829— Key to the Elementary Class-Book, *n. d.*—Ollendorff (H. G.) Italian Grammar, *Frankfort*, 1853—Noel et Chapsal Grammaire Française, *Paris*, 1870 ; and various School-Books   *a bundle*

367 Dibdin (T. F.) Poems, *half morocco, uncut, top edge gilt*
1797

*** Very scarce, as nearly the entire impression was destroyed by the Author.

368 Dibdin (T. F.) History of Cheltenham and its Environs, LARGE PAPER, *view, half red morocco, Cheltenham*, 1803

369 Dibdin (T. F.) Introduction to Greek and Latin Classics, Lexicons and Grammars, Bibles and Testaments, *second edition, half calf gilt*   1804

370 Dibdin. Another copy, LARGE PAPER, *one of the two copies with the plates taken off as duplicates on india paper, olive morocco extra, tooled leather joints, g. e.* 1804

371 Dibdin (T. F.) Translation of Fenelon's Treatise on the Education of Daughters, *frontispiece, half morocco extra, uncut, top edge gilt*   *Cheltenham*, 1805

372 Dibdin (T. F.) The Director, 2 vol. *half red morocco, uncut, top edges gilt*   1807

373 Dibdin (T. F.) Account of the first printed Psalters, 1807— Book Rarities, *only 36 copies printed*, 1811, *with various Catalogues added at end, red morocco extra, g. e. in* 1 *vol.*

374 Dibdin (T. F.) Edition of Sir T. More's Utopia, with Biographical and Bibliographical Introduction, 2 vol. *portrait, red morocco, gilt edges*   1808

375 Dibdin (T. F.) Bibliomania, FIRST EDITION, *presentation copy to Richard Heber, half red morocco, uncut, top edge gilt* 1809

376 Dibdin (T. F.) Specimen of an English De Bure, *presentation copy to J. M. Gutch with author's autograph inscription, half red morocco, uncut, top edge gilt, by H. Wood* 1810

*** Only 50 copies printed.

377 Dibdin (T. F.) Bibliography, a Poem, *only 50 copies printed, half red morocco, uncut, top edge gilt* 1812

378 DIBDIN (T. F.) BIBLIOTHECA SPENCERIANA, 4 vol. *fine engravings, maroon morocco extra, gilt edges, by C. Lewis,* 1814-15—ÆDES ALTHORPIANÆ and Supplement to Bibliotheca Spenceriana, 2 vol. *fine portraits and plates, olive morocco extra, gilt edges, by C. Lewis,* 1822— CASSANO CATALOGUE and Index, *olive morocco extra, gilt edges, by C. Lewis,* 1823 7 vol.

379 DIBDIN (T. F.) BIBLIOGRAPHICAL DECAMERON, 3 vol. *beautiful engravings, green morocco extra, leather joints, gilt edges* 1817

380 DIBDIN (T. F.) BIBLIOGRAPHICAL, ANTIQUARIAN AND PICTURESQUE TOUR IN FRANCE AND GERMANY, 3 vol. *portraits and numerous beautiful plates, with autograph letter of Dr. Dibdin added, russia extra, gilt edges, by C. Lewis* 1821

381 Dibdin. The same, Second Edition, 3 vol. *portraits and plates* 1829

382 Dibdin (T. F.) Library Companion, 2 vol. in 1, LARGE PAPER, *half green morocco, gilt edges* 1825

383 Dibdin (T. F.) Introduction to Greek and Latin Classics, Bibles and Fathers, *fourth edition, half russia extra,* 1827

384 Dibdin (T. F.) Edition of Thomas a Kempis' Imitation of Christ, with Introduction and Notes, *frontispiece and plates of Da Vinci's Last Supper of Our Lord, half morocco, uncut, top edge gilt* 1828

385 Dibdin (T. F.) Bibliophobia, *half red morocco, uncut, top edge gilt* 1832

386 Dibdin (T. F.) Lent Lectures, 2 vol. 1833

387 Dibdin (T. F.) Reminiscences of a literary Life, with Index, 2 vol. *portrait and plates, half red morocco, uncut, top edges gilt* 1836

388 DIBDIN (T. F.) BIBLIOGRAPHICAL, ANTIQUARIAN AND PICTURESQUE TOUR IN THE NORTHERN COUNTIES OF ENGLAND AND IN SCOTLAND, 2 vol. *fine engravings, half green morocco, uncut, top edges gilt* 1838

389 Dibdin (T. F.) Bibliomania, *illustrated with cuts, olive morocco extra, gilt edges, by Wickwar* 1842

390 Dibdin (T. F.) Cranmer, a Tale of modern Times, 3 vol. *uncut* 1843

391 Dibdin (T. F.) History of Dover, Autographs of Doctor and Miss Dibdin, *Reprinted for private distribution, n. d.*

392 Dibdin (T. F.) Lincolne Nosegay, *only 36 copies printed, morocco extra, gilt edges* n. d.

393 Dibdin (T. F.) Introduction to the Greek and Latin Classics, FIRST EDITION, *Glocester*, 1802 — Second Edition with Bibles, Lexicons and Grammars, 2 vol. *facsimile, calf, with Wodhull arms in gold on sides,* 1808—Harwood (E.) Editions of Greek and Latin Classics, *calf, with Wodhull arms in gold on sides,* 1790 (4)

394 Dibdin (T. F.) Lettre IX relative à la Bibliothèque de Rouen traduite avec des Notes par T. Licquet, *Paris*, 1821—Lettre XXX concernant l'Imprimerie et la Librairie de Paris traduite avec des Notes par G. A. Crapelet, *ib.* 1821, *half red morocco, uncut, t. e. g.* 2 vol.

395 Dickens (C.) Cricket on the Hearth, FIRST EDITION, *illustrations by Maclise, Doyle, Leech, &c. original cloth, soiled copy* 1846

396 Dickens (C.) Christmas Stories, *in 1 vol. half calf gilt* 1855-67

397 Dickens (C.) Mystery of Edwin Drood, FIRST EDITION, *portrait and 12 illustrations by S. L. Fildes, half calf gilt* 1870

398 Dickens (C.) Plays and Poems, with a few Miscellanies in Prose, 2 vol. 1885

399 Dickens (C.) Martin Chuzzlewit, *frontispiece,* 1850— American Notes, 1850—Sketches, *calf extra, Leipzig,* 1843—Hunted Down, *half calf extra, ib.* 1860—Pickwick Papers, *illustrations by Billinghame, Leeds, n. d.*— Nicholas Nickleby, 8 *illustrations, n. d.*—Barnaby Rudge and Reprinted Pieces, 2 vol. in 1, *plates, n. d.*— Great Expectations and Tale of two Cities, 2 vol. in 1, *frontispieces, n. d.*—Pic-Nic Papers, *n. d.* (9)

400 Dictionnaire des Cardinaux, *half red morocco, Paris,* 1857

401 Dionis Chrysostomi Orationes LXXX, Græce, *title and index mended, calf extra, gilt edges*
Venetiis, F. Turrisanus (Aldus), s. a. (1551)
*** The rarest of the Aldine Series printed for Turrisanus. Sir J. Thorold's copy sold for £3 17s. 6d.

402 Digby (K. H.) Compitum, 7 vol. *calf extra, uncut, top edges gilt* 1848-54

403 DIGBY (KENELM HENRY) BROAD STONE OF HONOUR, 5 vol. LARGE PAPER (*only 50 copies printed*), *plates, with autograph letter of author added, half morocco extra, uncut, top edges gilt* 1876-77

404 Digby (Kenelm Henry) Works, viz. Broad Stone of Honour, 1822—Lovers' Seat, 2 vol. 1856—Children's Bower, 2 vol. 1858—Evening on the Thames, 2 vol. 1860—The Chapel of St. John, 1863—Short Poems, 1866—Day on the Muses Hill, 1867—Hours with the first falling Leaves, 1868—Little low Bushes: Poems, 1869 — Halcyon Hours: Poems, 1870 — Ouranogaia, 2 vol. 1872—Last Year's Leaves, 1873—Temple of Memory, 1875, *tree-marbled calf extra, by Wilson*, 17 *vol.*

405 Digby (Sir K.) Private Memoirs, with the suppressed Passages, *portrait, half brown morocco, uncut, top edge gilt* 1827

406 Dobree (P. P.) Adversaria edente J. Scholefield, 2 vol. *calf gilt* *Cantab.* 1831-33

407 Douglas (Mrs. Stair) Life and Correspondence of W. Whewell, Master of Trinity College, Cambridge, *portrait* 1882

408 Drummond (H.) Natural Law in the Spiritual World 1883

409 Drury (Henry) Library Catalogue, *printed on writing paper (limited to 35 copies), MS. prices and names, half russia* 1827

410 Duckett (Sir G. F.) Record Evidences of the Abbey of Cluni *Lewes, privately printed*, 1886

411 Dunton (J.) Life and Errors, 2 vol. *portrait* 1818

412 Durandus (Bp. W.) Symbolism of Churches and Church Ornaments, with Essay, Notes and Illustrations by J. M. Neale and B. Webb, *Leeds*, 1849—Didron (M.) Christian Iconography, vol. I, 1851 (2)

413 Durer (Albert) Humiliation and Exaltation of Our Redeemer, 32 *facsimiles of the original wood-blocks* 1856

414 Dyce (Rev. A.) Recollections of the Table-Talk of S. Rogers and Porsoniana, *with portion of Dyce's autograph letter to Burges respecting Porsoniana added* 1856

415 EARLY ENGLISH TEXT SOCIETY'S PUBLICATIONS, 97 vol. (43 vol. in 25, *half red morocco, the rest unbound*), 1864-91—EXTRA SERIES, 59 vol. *uncut*, 1867-91

416 Ecclesiologist, First Series, published by Cambridge Camden Society, 3 vol. *plates, uncut, Cambridge*, 1843-44—New Series, published by the Ecclesiological Society, 23 vol. *plates* (15 vol. *half calf gilt, rest uncut*), *ib.* 1845-65 26 *vol.*

417 Edinburgh Gazetteer, 6 vol. *calf gilt* 1827

418 Edward II. A Poem on his Times, edited by Rev. C. Hardwick, *half morocco, uncut, top edge gilt* *printed for Percy Society*, 1849

419 Edwards (E.) Lives of the Founders of the British Museum, 2 vol. 1870

420 Eliot (Geo.) The Mill on the Floss, 3 vol. FIRST EDITION, *half morocco, gilt top* 1860

421 Ellicott (Bp. C. J.) Historical Lectures on the Life of Our Lord, *autograph letter of author added* 1861

422 Elliott (Grace D.) Journal of my Life during the French Revolution, *portrait* 1859

423 Elmsley (P.) Collection of 26 Reviews and critical Dissertations cut from various Periodicals, *half russia*
in 1 *vol.*

424 English Hexameter Translations from Schiller, Göthe, Homer, Callinus and Meleager 1847

425 English Historical Society's Publications, 23 vol. in 22, *all half bound red morocco, except 2 vol. of Bede, which are half bound calf* 1838-56

426 English Review, from April, 1844, to January, 1853, inclusive, 18 vol. (*vol. I to VIII half russia, and the rest in cloth*) 1844-53

427 Epistolæ Herberti de Losinga primi Episcopi Norwicensis, Osberti de Clara et Elmeri Prioris Cantuariensis editæ a R. Anstruther *Bruxellis,* 1846

428 Erckmann-Chatrian (MM.) Histoire d'un Paysan, 1789-92, 2 vol. *Paris,* 1869—Madame Thérèse, *ib. s. d.*—Le Fou Yegof, *ib. s. d.* 4 *vol.*

429 Essayists (British), with Prefaces, by A. Chalmers, 45 vol. *portraits, tree-marbled calf* 1808

430 EURIPIDIS TRAGŒDIÆ, Græce, 2 vol. FIRST EDITION *of* 14 *of the Tragedies, red morocco, gilt edges, with anchor in gold on sides* *Venetiis, Aldus,* 1503
⁎ Very rare. Mr. Beckford's copy sold for £11 10s. and Sir J. Thorold's for £9 9s.

431 Euripidis Hecuba et Iphigenia in Aulide D. Erasmo Interprete. Ejusdem (Erasmi) Ode de Laudibus Britanniæ Regisque Henrici VII ac regiorum Liberorum ejus ; et ejusdem Ode de Senectutis Incommodis *ib.* 1507
⁎ Scarce. Sir J. Thorold's copy sold for £2 18s.

432 Euripidis Scholia Græca ab Arsenio Achiepiscopo Monæbasiæ collecta, *calf, gilt edges*
Venetiis, L. A. Junta, 1534

433 Euripidis Electra, Græce, FIRST EDITION, *red morocco, gilt edges* *Romæ,* 1545
⁎ Very rare. Sir M. Sykes's copy sold for £5 12s. 6d.

434 Euripidis Electra, Græce et Latine, *vellum* *s. l.* 1546

435 Euripidis Alcestis, Gr. cum Notis J. H. Monk, *calf gilt*
            Cantab. 1816
*** Extremely rare, being one of the very few copies issued
 with the famous error *persentibunt* in the note on
 line 751.
436 EURIPIDIS OPERA OMNIA, Gr. et Lat. cum Scholiis
 Græcis et Notis variorum, 9 vol. LARGE PAPER, *bust,*
 orange morocco extra, gilt edges, with crest and motto of
 Earl of Gosford stamped in gold inside the covers
           Glasguæ, 1821
437 Euripidis Iphigenia ín Aulide, Græce edente J. Monk,
 LARGE PAPER, *half russia, uncut, t. e. g. Cantab.* 1840
438 Euripidis Fabulæ IV (Hippolytus, Alcestis, Iphigenia in
 Aulide et Iphigenia in Tauris), Græce cum Notis J. H.
 Monk, LARGE PAPER, *autograph letter of Bp. Monk*
 added, uncut   *ib.* 1857
   *** Only 14 copies printed.
439 Euripidis Alcestis, Andromache et Electra Græce edente
 T. Gaisford, 3 vol. in 1, *calf gilt, Oxon.* 1806-7-8—
 Opera omnia, Græce, 3 vol. *ib.* 1852   (4)
440 Euripidis Bacchæ, Heraclidæ et Medea, Gr. recensente P.
 Elmsley, 2 vol. *half russia, gilt edges, Oxonii,* 1821-28—
 Sophoclis Œdipus Tyrannus et Œdipus Coloneus ex
 Recensione P. Elmsley cum Notis suis et Variorum,
 2 vol. in 1, *russia, gilt edges, ib.* 1825 et 1823 (3)
441 Euripidis Bacchæ, in Greek, with Notes, by J. E. Sandys,
 numerous illustrations from works of ancient art, Cam-
 bridge, 1885—Andromache Græce cum Notis A. Mat-
 thiæ, *Oxon.* 1825—Phœnissæ, Gr. et Lat. ab H. Grotio,
 Paris, 1630—Andromacha Latine cum Q. Sept. Flo-
 rentis Christiani Notatis, *Lugd. Bat.* 1594   (4)
442 Eusebii Pamphili Eclogæ Propheticæ, Græce, edente T.
 Gaisford, *facsimile, Oxonii,* 1842—Contra Hieroclem et
 Marcellum Libri, Gr. et Lat. edidit T. Gaisford, *ib.*
 1852   (2)
443 Eutropius cum Pæanii Metaphrasi Græca ; Messala Cor-
 vinus de Augusti Progenie ; Julius Obsequens de Pro-
 digiis et Anonymi Oratio funebris, Gr. et Lat. in Imp.
 Constant. Constantini M. Fil. cum Annotationibus T.
 Hearne, LARGE PAPER, *old calf, scarce* *Oxonii,* 1703
444 Eyssenhardt (F.) Historia Miscella, *calf gilt*
              Berolini, 1869
445 Faber (F. W.) Sights and Thoughts in Foreign Churches
 and among Foreign Peoples   1842
446 Faber (F. W.) Life and Letters, by J. E. Bowden, *por-*
 trait   1869
447 Fabricii (J. A.) Codex Apocryphus Novi Testamenti,
 2 vol. in 1, *vellum*   *Hamburgi,* 1703
        D

448 Facetiæ Cantabrigienses, *portrait of Porson* 1836
449 Facetiæ. Carey (H.) Chrononhotonthologus, 1806, & Dragon of Wantley, *n. d.*—Gradus ad Cantabrigiam, *plates*, 1824 — Mathematogonia Græce, *Camb.* 1839—Puppet-Showman's Album, *illustrations by Gavarni, n. d. ;* and other Tracts in the volume, *half calf gilt*
450 Fenelon (M. de) Avantures de Telemaque, 2 vol. LARGE PAPER, *portrait and plates,* 1738—Aimé Martin (L.) Education des Mères de Famille, *calf extra, Paris,* 1841 —Pascal (B.) Lettres Provinciales, *portrait, gilt vellum, ib.* 1846 (4)
451 Ferguson (A.) History of the Roman Republic, 5 vol. *maps, calf extra* *Edinb.* 1825
452 Ferrigni (P. C.) Su a Giù per Firenze, *Firenze,* 1879— Guiducci (T.) Biografia di Donatello, *view of Florence Cathedral, ib.* 1887 — Dino Compagni Cronaca Fiorentina, *Milano,* 1837—Malespini (R. e G.) Storia Fiorentina, *ib.* 1876 — Garibaldi, Memorie autobiografiche, *Firenze,* 1888—Pellico (S.) Mie Prigioni, 1835—Cellini (B.) Vita, 2 parts, *Venezia,* 1844 (8)
453 Fielding (H.) Works, with Life by T. Roscoe, *portrait and illustrations by G. Cruikshank* 1851
454 Finlay (G.) History of Greece, from the Conquest by the Romans to the present Time (B.C. 146 to A.D. 1864) 7 vol. *portrait, autograph letter of author added* *Oxford,* 1877
455 Florence Miscellany, *tree-marbled calf extra, top edge gilt, by Wilson* *Florence,* 1785

*** Only a few copies printed, at the expense of Mrs. Piozzi, for presents, and now very scarce. Roscoe's copy sold for £4 16s. and Mr. Beckford's for £3 10s.

456 Florus et Lucius Ampelius, *Amst. D. Elzevir,* 1664— Justinus, *ib.* 1664—Velleius Paterculus, *ib.* 1664, *calf extra* *3 vol.*
457 Ford (J.) Gospel of St. Matthew illustrated from ancient and modern Authors, 1848—Chapter in English Church History, being the Minutes of the Society for promoting Christian Knowledge for 1698-1704, edited by E. McClure, *frontispiece,* 1888—Powell (W. S.) Discourses, *Bp. C. J. Blomfield's copy, with his autograph note and book-plate,* 1776—The Roman Catholic Question, a Series of important Documents on the Reestablishment of the Catholic Hierarchy in England, *full-length portrait of Cardinal Wiseman,* 1851—Melvill (H.) Cambridge Sermons, 2 vol. in 1, *half calf gilt,* 1836-40— Churton (W. R.) Defence of the English Ordinal, 1872 (6)

458 Foscolo (Ugo) Ultime Lettere di Jacopo Ortis, 2 vol.
THICK PAPER (*only 12 copies printed*), *2 portraits, pre-sentation copy to Roger Wilbraham, with author's autograph inscription, red morocco extra, gilt edges* 1817

459 Foss (E.) Tabulæ Curiales of Westminster Hall 1865

460 France (Archdeacon F.) Charges to Ely Clergy, *privately printed, with author's autograph inscription*, 1860-61—Browne (E. H.) Pentateuch and Elohistic Psalms, in Reply to Colenso, 1863 ; and 19 other Theological Tracts in the volume, *half calf gilt* 1860-66

461 Freeman (E. A.) Historical Essays, *with long autograph letter* (10 *pages*) *added, cloth, uncut* 1871

462 Freeman (E. A.) History of the Norman Conquest of England, 6 vol. *maps, with 2 autograph letters from the author added, Oxford*, 1867-79 — Reign of William Rufus and Accession of Henry I, 2 vol. *ib.* 1882 ; and 2 others (10)

463 Freeman (E. A.) Remarks on the Nomenclature of Gothic Architecture, *Oxford*, 1849; and 13 other Tracts by Freeman in the volume, *half calf gilt*

464 Frere (Rt. Hon. J. H.) Works, with Life by Sir B. Frere, 3 vol. *portrait and bust, with autograph letter of R. Shilleto added, tree-marbled calf extra, gilt edges, by Cecil and Larkin* 1874

465 Froude (R. H.) Remains, 4 vol. *half green morocco*
Lond. 1838, *and Derby*, 1839

466 Fullarton (Lady G.) Grantley Manor, *Paris*, 1847—Ellen Middleton, Lady-Bird and Stormy Life, 5 vol. in 3, *half calf extra, Leipzig*, 1846-53-67 (4)

467 Fuseli (H.) Life and Writings, 3 vol. *portrait, half calf extra* 1831

468 Gairdner (J.) Life of Richard III and Story of Perkin Warbeck, *portrait*, 1878—Clifford (E.) Life of Edward I, *portrait*, 1872 (2)

469 Gaisford (T.) Lectiones Platonicæ e Membranis Bodleianis, *half russia, Oxonii*, 1820—Ruhnkenii (D.) Dictata in Terentium, *half calf gilt, Bonnæ*, 1825—D'Orville (J. P.) Critica Vannus in inanes J. C. Pavonis Paleas, *vellum, Amst.* 1737—Jacobs (F.) Lectiones Stobenses, *half calf gilt, Jenæ*, 1827 (4)

470 Galfredi Monumetensis Historia Britonum edente J. A. Giles 1844

471 Gentleman's Magazine, from July 1843 to December 1862 inclusive, *not quite consecutive*, 21 vol. *various bindings* 1843-62

472 Gentleman's Magazine Library, 12 vol. *half morocco, uncut, top edges gilt* 1883-91

473 Gerard (Father J.) Narrative of the Gunpowder Plot, with
Life by J. Morris 1872
474 Gibbon (E.) History of the Decline and Fall of the Roman
Empire, 12 vol. *portrait, red morocco extra, g. e.* 1820
475 Gifford (W.) Baviad and Mæviad, *half morocco, uncut, top
edge gilt*, 1811—Anacreon, translated by T. Moore, 2 vol.
portraits, calf gilt, 1806—Wordsworth (W.) The Recluse,
1888—Book of Ballads, by Bon Gaultier, *illustrations by
A. Crowquill*, 1845—Dante's Vision of Hell, translated
by C. B. Cayley, 1851 (6)
476 Giraldus Cambrensis de Instructione Principum, 1846—
Chronicon Monasterii de Bello, 1846—Liber Eliensis,
vol. I, *with autograph letter of N. E. Hamilton added,*
1848 3 *vol.*
477 Glaisher (J.), E. Flammarion, W. de Fonvielle and G.
Tissandier, Travels in the Air, edited by J. Glaisher,
118 *illustrations* 1871
478 Glasse (G. H.) Masoni Caractacus et Miltoni Samson
Agonistes, Græco Carmine redditi cum Versione Latina,
2 vol. *half calf gilt* Oxonii, 1781-88
479 Goethe (J. W. von) Werke. Auswahl, 12 vol. *Stuttgart,*
1867—Schiller (F. von) Gedichte, 2 vol. *frontispiece,
Leipzig,* 1818; and 12 others, German (26)
480 Goodman (Bp. G.) Court of James I, 2 vol. *portraits of
Q. Elizabeth and James I, calf extra* 1839
481 Goodwin (G.) Catalogue of the Harsnett Library at Col-
chester, *frontispiece, presentation copy, with letter signed
by H. C. Wanklyn, Town Clerk* 1888
₊ Only 250 copies privately printed for presents.

482 Gordon (A. H.) Letters and Notes written during the
Disturbances in the Highlands (known as the "Devil
Country") of Viti Levu, Fiji, 1876, 2 vol. *autograph
letter of author added* Edinb. 1879
₊ Privately printed for presents only.

483 Gordon (P. L.) Personal Memoirs, 2 vol. *portrait* 1830
484 Gordon (T.) Cordial for low Spirits, 3 vol. 1751-63—
Southey (R.) Espriella's Letters from England, 3 vol.
1808—Dutens (L.) Memoirs of a Traveller now in
Retirement and Dutensiana, 5 vol. 1806—Moore (T.)
The World at Westminster, 2 vol. in 1, 1816 (12)
485 Gray (T.) Poems, LARGE PAPER, *Du Roveray's edition,
plates, green morocco, gilt edges* 1800
486 Gray (T.) Elegia tradotta in più Lingue per Cura del
Dottore A. Torri, *half calf gilt, uncut* Livorno, 1843
₊ Containing English Text, with Versions in Italian,
Latin, Hebrew, French and German by various Poets.

487 Greek Tragic Theatre, containing Æschylus by Dr. Potter, Sophocles by Dr. Francklin, and Euripides by M. Wodhull, 5 vol. *old calf extra* 1809

488 Green (J. R.) Short History of the English People, *maps and tables* 1874

489 Green (J. R.) Short History of the English People, 1874 —Armitage (Ella S.) Childhood of the English Nation, 1877—Keightley (T.) History of Rome, 1837—Corner (Julia) Question on History of Europe, 1837—Markham (Mrs.) History of France, 2 vol. 1830 (6)

490 Gregorii IX Decretales Epistolæ *Paris.* 1541

491 Gregorii Nazanzeni (S.) Tragœdia Christus Patiens, Græce, *green morocco extra, gilt edges, very scarce Romæ, A. Bladus (Typis Aldinis),* 1542

492 Gregorii Turonici Historia Francorum, *Paris.* 1561 — Adonis Chronica, *slightly wormed, ib.* 1561 *in* 1 *vol.*

493 Gregorovius (F.) Storia della Città di Roma (403-1534) con Indice, 9 vol. *half gilt vellum, Venezia,* 1866-76— Lucrezia Borgia, *portrait, gilt vellum, Firenze,* 1874— Urbano VIII, *half gilt vellum, Roma,* 1879 (11)

494 Gregorovius (F.) Le Tombe dei Papi, *Roma,* 1879— Bonghi (R.) Pio IX e il Papa futuro, *Milano,* 1877— Gregorovius (F.) Ricordi Storici e pittorici d'Italia, 2 vol. *Milano,* 1877 — Hock (C. F.) Gerberto (Silvestro II) ed il suo Secolo, *ib.* 1846—Potthast (A.) Regesti de' Romani Pontefici (1198-1304), *Roma,* 1874 (6)

495 Gregory (D. F.) Examples of Differential and Integral Calculus, *Cambridge,* 1841—Application of Analysis to solid Geometry, by D. F. Gregory and W. Walton, *ib.* 1845 2 *vol.*

496 Gregory (D. F.) Mathematical Writings, edited by W. Walton, with Life by R. L. Ellis, *portrait, Camb.* 1865 —O'Brien (M.) Plane Co-ordinate Geometry, *ib.* 1844 —Herschel (J. F. W.) Examples of Calculus of Finite Differences, *ib.* 1820 — Besant (W. H.) on Roulettes and Glissettes, *ib.* 1870—Moon (R.) Fresnel and his Followers, &c. *ib.* 1849—Newton (Sir I.) First three Sections of Principia, edited by J. H. Evans, *ib.* 1843 ; and 8 others (14)

497 Gresley (W.) Portrait of an English Churchman, *MS. notes, proving it opposed to Prayer-Book, half calf gilt* 1839

498 Greswell (W. P.) Memoirs of Politianus, J. Picus of Mirandula, Sannazarius, Bembus, Fracastorius, Flaminius and Amalthei, with Translations from their poetical Works, *calf extra, with arms of H. N. Evans in gold on sides Manchester,* 1805

499 Greswell (E.) View of the early Parisian Greek Press,
2 vol. *half russia extra*   *Oxford*, 1833

500 Grey (Z.) Life of T. Baker, with Catalogue of his MS.
Collections by R. Masters, *Bp. C. J. Blomfield's copy,
with his book-plate, old calf*   *Cambridge*, 1784

501 Grier (R. M.) Memoir of Julia Allen, *portrait and etching
by Thackeray, autograph letters of Allen and Grier added*
1889

502 Grossetete (Bp. R.) Carmina Anglo-Normanica, edited by
M. Cooke   1852

503 Guizot (M.) Washington, translated by H. Reeve, *calf
extra*   1840

504 Gunning (H.) Reminiscences of Cambridge University,
Town and Country, 2 vol. *portrait*   1854

505 Hall (P.) The Crypt, 3 vol. *half calf, Ringwood*, 1827-28

506 Hamilton (Lady) Memoirs, *portrait by Romney, half calf
extra, gilt edges*   1815

507 Hamilton (Comte A.) Contes, 2 vol. *Paris*, 1813—
Œuvres diverses, *ib.* 1813—Memoires du Comte de
Grammont, 2 vol. *ib.* 1812, *French red morocco, borders
of gold, gilt edges*   5 *vol.*

508 Hampson (R. T.) Medii Ævi Kalendarium, 2 vol. *facsimiles, half morocco*   1841

509 Hardwick (C.) Christ and other Masters, 4 Parts
Camb. 1855-59

510 Hardy (Sir T. D.) Description of the Patent Rolls, with
Itinerary of King John   1835

511 Hardy (Sir T. D.) Description of the Close Rolls, *calf
extra, gilt edges, printed for private circulation*, 1833—
Report XXVIII on Public Records, 1867   (2)

512 Hardy (Sir T. D.) Report upon Venetian Archives   1866

513 Hare (J. C.) Fragments of Two Essays in English
Philology, *Camb.* 1873—Skeat (W. W.) English Words
found in Norman French and only English Proclamation
of Henry III, 1882—Tewin-Water, or Story of Lady
Cathcart, *Enfield*, 1876—Country Spectator, 33 Nos. in
1 vol. *Gainsborough*, 1792-93—Jaques (J.) History of
Junius and his Works, 1843—Report on Carte and
Carew Papers, 1864   (6)

514 Hare (J. C.) Vindication of Luther, 1855—Robertson
(J. C.) How shall we conform to the English Liturgy?
1844—Wood (E. G.) Regal Power of the Church, *Cambridge*, 1888—Bickersteth (E. H.) Rock of Ages,
author's autograph inscription, Hampstead, 1859—Cazenove (J. G.) Aspects of the Reformation, *author's
autograph letter added*, 1869—Westcott (P. F.) Victory
of the Cross, *Cambridge*, 1888   (6)

515 Hartshorne (C. H.) Book-Rarities in Cambridge University, *plates, calf extra* 1829
516 Haydn (J.) Book of Dignities 1851
517 Head (Sir F. B.) Bubbles from the Brunnen of Nassau,
Darmstadt, 1870 — Black's Tourist in Scotland, *maps
and plates, Edinb.* 1863-64—Dickens (C.) Dictionary of
London, 1879—Irish Tourist's Handbook, *maps and
plates,* 1852 ; and other Guide-Books, *and maps, a bundle*
518 Headley (H.) Select Beauties of Ancient English Poetry,
with Life by Rev. H. Kett, 2 vol. *red morocco extra, gilt
edges* 1810

HEARNE'S PUBLICATIONS.

519 Livii Historiæ edente T. Hearne, 6 vol. LARGE PAPER, *old
calf* *Oxonii,* 1708
  ₊ Scarce. The Towneley copy sold for £4 8s.
520 Dodwell (H.) de Parma equestri. Accedit T. Neli Dialogus
inter Reginam Elizabetham et Comitem Leycestriæ de
Academiæ Oxoniensis Ædificiis, edente T. Hearne,
LARGE PAPER, *plates, red morocco, gilt edges* *ib.* 1713
  ₊ Very scarce having been prohibited. Dent's copy sold
for £13 13s.
521 Aluredi Beverlacensis Annales edente T. Hearne *ib.* 1716
  ₊ Scarce. The Towneley copy sold for £6 16s. 6d.
522 Camdeni (G.) Annales Rerum Anglicarum et Hibernicarum
regnante Elizabetha edente T. Hearne, 3 vol. LARGE
PAPER, *portrait, red morocco, Harleian gold tooling*
ib. 1717
  ₊ Scarce. Edwards's copy sold for £13.
523 Guilielmi Neubrigensis Historia curante T. Hearne, 3 vol.
LARGE PAPER, *red morocco, Harleian gold tooling, gilt
edges, rebacked* *ib.* 1719
  ₊ This copy sold for £14 14s. in the Duke of Grafton's
sale.
524 Sprotti Chronica et alia Opuscula edente T. Hearne, *calf
gilt, with Lord Aylesbury's crest on sides* *ib.* 1719
  ₊ Duke of Grafton's copy sold for £4 14s. 6d.
525 Hearne. Sprotti (T.) Chronica edente T. Hearne *ib.* 1719
526 Roberti de Avesbury Historia Edvardi III. Accedunt
libri Saxonici qui ad Manus J. Joscelini venerunt et
Nomina Scriptorum Historiæ Anglorum per J. Joscelinum
edente T. Hearne *ib.* 1720
  ₊ Duke of Roxburghe's copy sold for £3 3s.
527 Collection of curious Discourses by eminent Antiquaries,
published by T. Hearne, LARGE PAPER, *portrait of
Hearne, red morocco, borders of gold, g. e. Oxford,* 1720
  ₊ Sir M. Sykes's copy sold for £5 5s.

HEARNE'S PUBLICATIONS—*continued.*

528 Textus Roffensis. Accedunt Angliæ Episcoporum Formulæ de Canonica Obedientia Archiepiscopis Cantuar-
iensibus præstanda et L. Hutteni Dissertatio Anglice
conscripta de Antiquitatibus Oxoniensibus edente T.
Hearne, LARGE PAPER, *calf gilt* *Oxonii*, 1720
*** Scarce. Bindley's copy sold for £9.

529 Fordun (Johannis de) Scotichronicon cum Supplemento et
Continuatione edidit T. Hearnius, 5 vol. LARGE PAPER,
plates, calf gilt *ib.* 1722
*** Scarce. The Duke of Grafton's copy sold for £15 15s.

530 History and Antiquities of Glastonbury (by Eyston),
edited by T. Hearne, LARGE PAPER, *plates, calf gilt*
Oxford, 1722
*** Very scarce. Bindley's copy sold for £14 3s. 6d.

531 Johannis Glastoniensis Chronica edente T. Hearne, 2 vol.
LARGE PAPER, *old calf* *Oxonii*, 1726
*** Scarce. Duke of Grafton's copy sold for £19 18s. 6d.

532 Thomæ de Elmham Vita et Gesta Henrici V, edente T.
Hearne, LARGE PAPER, *old gilt calf* *ib.* 1727
*** Scarce. The Duke of Grafton's copy sold for £11 11s.

533 Johannis de Trokelowe Annales Edvardi II ; Henrici de
Blaneforde Cronica ; et Edvardi II Vita a Monacho
Malmesburiensi &c. edente T. Hearne, LARGE PAPER,
calf gilt *ib.* 1729
*** Very scarce. The Duke of Grafton's copy sold for £21,
and Willett's for the same sum.

534 Walteri Hemingford Historia Edvardi I, Edvardi II et
Edvardi III, edente T. Hearne, 2 vol. LARGE PAPER,
*blue morocco, gilt edges, with Crest of Duke of Buccleugh
in gold on sides* *ib.* 1731
*** Very rare. The Towneley copy sold for £30 19s. 6d.

535 Hearne (T.) Vindication of the Oath of Allegiance, *portrait, calf gilt* 1731

536 Thomas Otterbourne et Johannes Whethamstede de Rebus
Anglicanis ab Origine Gentis usque ad Edvardum IV,
edente T. Hearne, 2 vol. LARGE PAPER, *old calf, ib.* 1732
*** Very scarce. The Duke of Grafton's copy sold for £21.

537 Chronicon Prioratus de Dunstaple cum Appendice, edidit
T. Hearne, 2 vol. *autograph notes of Browne Willis, half
red morocco* *ib.* 1733
*** Gough's copy sold for £5. and Dr. Luard in his MS.
Note states he gave £3 3s. for this.

538 Benedictus Abbas Petroburgensis de Vita et Gestis Hen-
rici II et Ricardi I edente T. Hearne, 2 vol. LARGE
PAPER, *calf extra, uncut, top edges gilt* *ib.* 1735
*** Very rare. Willett's copy sold for £25 4s.

539 Rossi Warwicensis (J.) Historia Regum Angliæ, edente
T. Hearne. Accedit J. Lelandi Nænia in Mortem H.
Duddelegi Equitis   *Oxonii*, 1745

540 Leland (J.) Itinerary and New Year's Gift with Discourse
of Antiquities found in Yorkshire, edited by T. Hearne,
9 vol. in 5, LARGE PAPER, *plates, old gilt calf*
Oxford, 1768-69
   ⁎ Sir M. Sykes's copy sold for £10 10s.

541 Liber Niger Saccarii, necnon Wilhelmi Worcestrii Annales
Rerum Anglicarum cum Præfatione et Appendice T.
Hearnii. Accedunt Chartæ antiquæ et Opuscula varia,
LARGE PAPER, *old calf*   *Londini*, 1774
   ⁎ Nassau's copy sold for £2 2s.

542 Leland (J.) de Rebus Britannicis Collectanea edente T.
Hearne, 6 vol. LARGE PAPER, *plates, old gilt tree-marbled
calf*   *ib.* 1774
   ⁎ Baker's copy sold for £7.

543 Robert of Gloucester and Peter Langtoft's Metrical Chronicles, edited by T. Hearne, 4 vol. *reprints of* 1724-25
editions, half red morocco   1810

544 Hearne (T.) Reliquiæ Hearnianæ, edited by P. Bliss,
2 vol. *portrait, half calf gilt, uncut*   *Oxford*, 1857

545 Hecker (J. F. C.) Epidemics of the Middle Ages and Child
Pilgrimages, translated by B. G. Babington   1859

546 Heine (H.) Buch der Lieder, *half calf gilt, Hamburg*, 1854
—Uhland (L.) Gedichte, *Stuttgart*, 1853—Rückert (F.)
Rostem und Suhrab, *ib.* 1846—Goethe (J. W. von)
Wahrheit und Dichtung, 3 vol. in 2, *half calf gilt, ib.*
1840; and 3 others, German   (8)

547 Hephæstion de Metris, Græce. Accedunt Terentianus
Maurus de Syllabis et Metris Latine et Procli Chresto-
mathia Grammatica Græce cum Notis T. Gaisford, 2 vol.
cloth, uncut   *Oxonii*, 1855

548 Herbert (G.) Works in Prose and Verse, 2 vol. *portrait
and view of Bemerton, Hulme Prize, calf extra, with arms
in gold on sides*   *W. Pickering*, 1846

549 Hermesianactis Fragmentum, Gr. Notis et Glossario et
Versionibus tum Latinis tum Anglicis instruxit J.
Bailey. Subjiciuntur Archilochi ac Pratinæ Fragmenta
duo similiter instructa. Accedit G. Burgesii Epistola
critica, *with editor's woeful autograph letter added*, 1839

550 Herodiani Historiæ Gr. et Lat. *morocco, Venetiis, Aldus,* 1524
   ⁎ Scarce. Sir M. Sykes's copy, which sold for £1 15s. in
his sale, was resold in Sir J. Thorold's for £3 15s.

551 Herodotus Græce cum Notis Variorum edente T. Gaisford,
4 vol. *calf gilt* *Oxonii*, 1824

552 Herodotus, Book I to III in Greek, with Notes by A. H.
Sayce, 1883—Thucydides, Book I in Greek, with Notes
by R. Shilleto, *with editor's autograph letter and can-*
celled preface added, *Cambridge*, 1872 — Æschyli
Eumenides Græce cum Notis G. Linwood, *half russia*,
Oxonii, 1844 (3)

553 Herodotus, Græce ex Recensione Baehr, 2 vol. *Oxon.*
1845—Sophocles Gr. ex Recensione Dindorfii, *ib.* 1844—
Æschylus ex Recensione Dindorfii, 1845—Anacreon et
Sapphus, Græce, *Amst.* 1807 — Theocritus, Bion et
Moschus Gr. 1560—Pindari Epinicia Gr. edente C. H.
Weise, *Lipsiæ*, 1845 (7)

554 Herrick (R.) Poetical Works, *portrait* 1859

555 Hessels (J. H.) Gutenberg, was he the Inventor of Printing?
MS. corrections, half morocco, uncut, top edge gilt. 1882

556 Hessels (J. H.) Haarlem the Birth-Place of Printing not
Mentz 1887

557 Hill (A. G.) Churches of Cambridgeshire 1880

558 Hind (J.) Algebra, *Cambridge*, 1839 — Snowball (J. C.)
Plane Trigonometry, *ib.* 1839 — Wood (J.) Algebra,
with additions by T. Lund, *ib.* 1841 — Murphy (R.)
Theory of Algebraical Equations, 1839—Wood (J.)
Mechanics, enlarged by J. C. Snowball, *Camb.* 1841;
and a volume of 11 Mathematical Tracts by Hopkins,
Pritchard, &c. *half calf gilt* 6 *vol.*

559 Hinton (E.) Life and Letters, *portrait*, 1878—Hutton
(R. H.) Essays on Modern Guides to Faith, 1887—
Hodson (W. S. R.) Hodson of Hodson's Horse, 1889 (3)

560 Historiæ Augustæ Scriptores cum Notis J. B. Egnatii,
stamped pigskin, with portraits of Justice and Chastity
stamped as centre ornaments, dated 1567
Venetiis, Aldus, 1519
₊ Sir J. Thorold's copy sold for £1 1s.

561 Historiæ Augustæ Scriptores cum Notis J. B. Egnatii,
calf *ib.* 1521
₊ Sir J. Thorold's copy sold for £1 10s.

562 Historical Pamphlets, viz.: Thorpe (B.) Correspondence relative to Publication of Materials of British History,
1864—Summa Conciliorum brevissima, *Romæ*, 1869—
Tozer (H. F.) Byzantine Satire and Franks in the
Peloponnese, *author's autograph inscriptions*, 1881-83;
and 17 other Tracts by Meyer, Weber, Schmitz, Liebermann, Jessop, Balzani, &c. in the volume, *half calf gilt*
1864-89

43

563 Hoare (Sir R. C.) Catalogue of Books relating to the History and Topography of Italy, collected in 1786-90, *autograph of Edward Hoare, half morocco, uncut,* 1812
₊ Very scarce, as only 12 copies were printed.

564 Hodson (G. H.) and E. Ford, History of Enfield, LARGE PAPER, *plates* *Enfield Press,* 1873
₊ Printed for Subscribers only and not published.

565 Hodson (Major W. S. R.) Hodson of Hodson's Horse, or Twelve Years of a Soldier's Life in India, LARGE PAPER, *photograph, half morocco, uncut, top edge gilt* 1883

566 Hodson. Another copy on small Paper, *no photograph, cloth* 1883

567 Holland (H. S.) Creed and Character, 1887—Williams (I.) Female Characters of Holy Scripture, 1859—Maurice (F. D.) on the Lord's Prayer, *Camb.* 1861 ; and 12 others, Religious (15)

568 Homeri Batrachomyomachia Græce ; Glossa Græca ; Variantibus Lectionibus, Versionibus Latinis, Commentariis et Indicibus illustrata a M. Maittaire, *fine copy, ruled, blue morocco extra, gilt edges* 1721

569 Homeri Hymnus in Cererem Græce editus a D. Ruhukenio et Latine versus a J. H. Vossio, FINE PAPER, *red morocco, gilt edges, Dr. Hawtrey's copy with his Bookplate* *Lugd. Bat.* 1808

570 Homeri Opera, Græce, cum Notis S. Clarkii Cura J. A. Ernesti qui et suas Notas adspersit, 5 vol. LARGE PAPER, *Lord Romilly's copy, russia extra, with arms in gold on sides* *Glasguæ,* 1814

571 Homeri Ilias et Odyssea, 2 vol. in 1, *portrait, russia, gilt edges* *Pickering,* 1831

572 Homilies, *Oxford,* 1844—Maclear (G. F.) History of Christian Missions during the Middle Ages, *Cambridge,* 1863—Maurice (F. D.) Prophets and Kings of the Old Testament, *ib.* 1853—Body (G.) Life of Temptation, 1873—Harris (Miss E. F. S.) Rest in the Church, 1848 (5)

573 HOOK (DEAN W. F.) LIVES OF THE ARCHBISHOPS OF CANTERBURY, WITH INDEX, 12 vol. *portrait and autograph letter of author added, cloth, uncut* 1860-76

574 Hope (Rt. Hon. A. J. B. Beresford) English Cathedrals of the XIXth Century, *with illustrations, autograph letter of the author added* 1861

575 Hope (Rt. Hon. A. J. B. Beresford) Worship in the Church of England, *"From the Author"* 1874

576 Hope (Rt. Hon. A. J. B. Beresford) Letters on Church Matters, 1851 ; and 12 other Tracts by Mr. Hope, 1860-71, *half calf gilt* *in 2 vol.*

577 Horæ intemeratæ Virginis Mariæ secundum Usum Romanæ Curiæ cum Calendario et Almanach (1513-29), PRINTED ON VELLUM, *with* MINIATURES *and* BORDERS *illuminated in gold and colours, wants title, and border of last leaf cut off, red velvet, gilt edges, sold with all faults*
Paris. 1513

578 HORATIUS. FIRST ALDINE EDITION, *old red morocco, gilt edges* *Venetiis, Aldus,* 1501

*** Extremely rare. Sir J. Thorold's copy sold for £30; the Wodhull and Earl of Crawford's each for £31 10s.

579 Horatii Poemata cum Notis A. Cuningamii, 2 vol. *frontispieces, Bp. C. J. Blomfield's copy with his Bookplate, vellum, Hagæ,* 1721—Horatius, *portrait, calf, Glasguæ, R. Foulis,* 1744—Virgilius, *Amst. Elzevir,* 1676—Terentius, *several leaves mended, Lugd. Bat. Elzevir,* 1635; and 2 others (7)

580 Horatii Opera illustrated from antique Gems, by C. W. King: the Text revised with Introduction by H. A. J. Munro, *woodcuts,* 1869—Horatii Opera, with Notes by C. Anthon, 1846 (2)

581 Horatius restitutus, by J. Tate, *red morocco extra, g. e.* 1837

582 Horne Tooke (J.) Diversions of Purley, *frontispiece* 1857

583 Hortus Animæ, or Garden of the Soul, *brown morocco extra, gilt edges, J. Philp, n. d.*—Paroissien Romain, *plates, blue morocco extra, leather joints, gilt linings, gilt edges, Paris, s. d.*—Nouveau Testament, *blue morocco, gilt edges, S. Bagster et Fils, s. d.* (3)

584 Host (F. J. A.) On Monogenes Theos and Eastern Creeds
Camb. 1876

585 Howitt (W.) Rural Life of England, 2 vol. *woodcuts,* 1838

586 Hume (D.) History of England with Continuation, by T. Smollett, 19 vol. *Cooke's Pocket Edition, with Portraits and historical Engravings, old calf* 1793-94

587 Hurtado de Mendoza (D.) Adventures of Lazarillo de Tormes, *plates* 1821

588 Hurter (F.) Storia del Sommo Pontifice Innocenzo III, e de' suoi Contemporanei tradotta dall' Ab. C. Rovida, 3 vol. *portrait, half vellum* *Milano,* 1839-40

589 Husenbeth (F. C.) Emblems of Saints, edited by A. Jessopp, *emblazoned coats of Saintly Arms, with autograph letter of Editor added, cloth, uncut, top edge gilt*
Norwich, 1882

590 Hymns ancient and modern, *with Tunes compiled and arranged by W. H. Monk, calf extra* *n. d.*

591 Inchbald (Mrs.) British Theatre, 25 vol. *character prints, calf* 1808

592 Hymers (J.) on Differential Equations and Calculus of finite Differences, *Cambridge,* 1839—Coombe (J. A.) Solutions of the Cambridge Problems for 1840-41, *ib.* 1841—Walton (W.) Solutions of the Problems and Riders for 1864, *ib.* 1864—De Morgan (A.) on Probabilities, 1838—Besant (W. H.) Conic Sections, *Camb.* 1869—Abbott (R.) Calculus of Variations, 1841—Fitton (Sarah Mary) First Steps to Astronomy and Geography, *plates,* 1828—La Lande (J. de) Tables de Logarithmes, *Bruxelles,* 1838 (8)

QUARTO.

593 DIGBY (K. H.) MORES CATHOLICI, or Ages of Faith, Eleven Books in 3 vol. LARGE PAPER, *half morocco, uncut, top edges gilt* 1844-48

594 DIOGENES LAERTIUS de Vitis, Dogmatibus et Apophthegmatibus clarorum Philosophorum Gr. et Lat. cum Notis Variorum edente M. Meibomio. Accedunt Æg-Menagii Observationes, &c. 2 vol. LARGE PAPER, *busts, fine copy in Dutch vellum* Amst. 1692

_{*} Scarce on Large Paper. Sir M. Sykes's copy sold for £6 5s.

595 Dixon (W. H.) Fasti Eboracences, or Lives of the Archbishops of York, enlarged by Rev. J. Raine, LARGE PAPER, *autograph letter of Raine added, red morocco extra, gilt edges, by Riviere* 1863

596 Dodgson (C. L.) Formulæ of Trigonometry, *Oxford,* 1861

597 Dutripon (F. P.) Concordantiæ Bibliorum Sacrorum Vulgatæ Editionis, *vellum* Paris. 1838

598 Ennii Fragmenta ab H. Columna conquisita et explicata recusa accurante T. Hesselio, *calf extra* Amst. 1707

599 Epistolæ Basilii Magni, Libanii, Chionis, Æschinis, Isocratis, Phalaridis, Bruti, Apollonii Tyanensis et Juliani Apostatæ, Græce Cura Aldi Manutii, FIRST EDITION, *red morocco, g. e. by Roger Payne, Venetiis, Aldus,* 1499

600 Esquiline (The) a monthly Magazine from November 1889 to May 1890, and from November 1890 to February 1891, and for May 1891, 12 Nos. *Rome,* 1889-91

601 EURIPIDIS TRAGŒDIÆ IV (Medea, Hippolytus, Alcestis et Andromache Græce cura J. Lascaris, FIRST EDITION, *printed in capital letters, very slightly wormed, else fine copy in vellum*
s. l. & a. sed Florentiæ per L. de Alopa, ante 1500

_{*} Extremely rare. Renouard's copy sold for £36 15s. and Wodhull's for £22 10s.

602 Euripidis Hippolytus et Phœnissæ, Gr. et Lat. cum Notis L. C. Valckenaer, 2 vol. *vellum* Lugd. Bat. 1768-1802

603 Evangelia IV et Acta Apostolorum, exact copy in ordinary
type of Bezæ Codex Cantabrigiensis, with Introduction,
Annotations and Facsimiles by F. H. Scrivener
Cambridge, 1864

604 Evangiles. Traduction nouvelle par H. Lasserre, *numerous
elegant illustrations, olive morocco extra, uncut, top edge
gilt, by Zaehnsdorf* *Paris*, 1888

605 Ezra. The missing Fragment of the Latin Translation of
the fourth Book, discovered and edited, with Introduction and Notes by R. L. Bensly, *facsimile, cloth, with
Trinity College arms in gold on sides* *Cambridge*, 1875

606 Fabricii (J. A.) Bibliotheca Latina mediæ et infimæ Ætatis
cum Supplemento C. Schœttgenii aucta a P. J. D.
Mausi, 6 vol. in 3, *old calf* *Patavii*, 1754

607 Fabyan (R.) New Chronicles of England and France, with
Preface and Index by Sir H. Ellis, *calf gilt* 1811

608 Fenn (Sir J.) Paston Letters, vol. V, *portrait and facsimiles, uncut* 1823

609 Field (F.) Otium Norvicense, Pars tertia *Oxford*, 1881

610 Fortunati (V. H. C. *Episcopi Pictaviensis*) Opera omnia
cum Vita Studio M. A. Luchi, 2 vol. *old calf, gilt edges,
with arms of Pius VI in gold on sides*, *Romæ*, 1786-87

611 Fosbrooke (T. D.) British Monachism, *numerous plates,
calf gilt* 1817

612 Franconis (Beati) Vita, in Latin and English Verse by A.
Rowan *Dublin*, 1858

613 Gaisford (T.) Codices MSS. et Impressi cum Notis MSS.
olim Dorvilliani et Catalogus Manuscriptorum E. D.
Clarke in Bibliotheca Bodleiana, 2 vol. in 1, *half russia*
Oxonii, 1806-12

614 Gale (R. and S.) Reliquiæ Galeanæ, 3 parts in 1, *plates,
russia* 1782-84

615 Galfredi Le Baker de Swynebroke Chronicon, edited, with
Notes, by E. M. Thompson, *facsimile* *Oxford*, 1889

616 Gams (P. B.) Series Episcoporum Ecclesiæ Catholicæ,
vellum *Ratisbonæ*, 1873

617 Gascoigne (T.) Loci e Libro Veritatum, illustrating the
Condition of Church and State, 1403-58, with Introduction by J. E. Thorold Rogers, *facsimile, MS. corrections
by Dr. Luard* *Oxford*, 1881

618 Gesenius's Hebrew Grammar enlarged by E. Rödiger,
translated by B. Davies, with Hebrew Reading Book by
the Translator, *russia extra* 1846

619 Gesenius (F. H. W.) Hebrew and Chaldee Lexicon, with
Additions by S. P. Tregelles 1847

620 Gibson (W. S.) History of Tynemouth Monastery, 2 vol. *illuminated plates and initial letters, and various views, half morocco, uncut* 1846-47

621 GNOMÆ MONOSTICHÆ ET MUSÆI HERO ET LEANDER, Græce, Cura J. Lascaris, FIRST EDITION, *printed in capital letters, fine copy in red morocco, borders of gold s. l. & a. sed Florentiæ, F. de Alopa,* 1494
  *** Excessively rare. The Duke of Grafton's copy sold for £43.

622 Gospels (Four), with Annotations by Bp. J. Lonsdale and Archdeacon W. H. Hale, 1849—Order and Method of the Bible, *charts, n. d.* (2)

623 Green (T.) Extracts from the Diary of a Lover of Literature, *half calf gilt, Ipswich,* 1810—Ford (J.) Memoir of T. Green of Ipswich, *portrait, only* 100 *copies printed for presents, ib.* 1825 (2)

624 Gregorii Nazianzeni Carmina, Gr. et Lat. *Errata mended, old green morocco* *Venetiis, Aldus,* 1504

625 Hamerton (P. G.) Contemporary French Painters, 16 *photographic illustrations on india paper, ornamented cloth, gilt edges* 1868

626 Hamilton Palace Collection, *illustrated priced catalogue, plates* 1882

627 Hardyng (J.) Chronicle (in Verse), with Continuation (in Prose) by R. Grafton. Edited, with Preface and Index, by Sir H. Ellis, *calf gilt* 1812

628 Hearne. Letters addressed to T. Hearne, edited by F. Ouvry, *half Roxburghe, uncut* 1874
  *** Privately printed for presents only.

629 Heliodori Historia Æthiopica, Græce, FIRST EDITION, *autograph of J. Toup and numerous MS. notes* *Basileæ,* 1534

630 Hessels (J. H.) Ecclesiæ Londino-Batavæ Tomus I, A. Ortelii et Virorum eruditorum ad eundem et ad J. Colium Ortelianum (A. Ortelii Sororis) Epistulæ, *portrait of A. Ortelius, Cantab.* 1887—Tomus II, Epistulæ et Tractatus cum Reformationis tum Ecclesiæ Londino-Batavæ Historiam illustrantes, *ib.* 1889, *uncut* 2 *vol.*

631 Hieroclis in aureos Versus Pythagoræ Opusculum J. Aurispa Interprete, *fine copy in vellum* *Romæ, A. Pannartz in Domo P. de Maximis,* 1475
  *** Valuable as a specimen of printing by Pannartz, after his separation from Sweynheim. The Solar copy sold for 161 francs.

632 Hill (G. W.) and W. H. Frere, Memorials of Stepney Parish, 4 parts, *map, plans and plates* *Guildford,* 1890-91

633 Hill (N.) Ancient Poem of Guillaume de Guileville, entitled " *Le Pelerinage de l'Homme*," compared with J. Bunyan's Pilgrim's Progress, *portrait of Bunyan and plates, ornamented cloth, uncut* 1858

634 Hogarth (W.) Works, with Comment by Rev. J. Trusler, 2 vol. *portrait and plates, with catalogue of works placed in British Institution for exhibition* 1814 *added, half calf gilt* 1833

635 Homeri Ilias et Odyssea Græce cura Grenvilliorum, 4 vol. in 2, *calf extra* *Oxonii,* 1800

636 Homeri Ilias, Editio Polyglotta (Græce, Latine, Italice, Gallice, Anglice, Hispanice et Germanice), 2 vol. *numerous plates, half vellum* *Firenze,* 1838

637 Innocent IV Registres par E. Berger, ·5 parts *Paris,* 1881-84

638 Jebb (R. C.) Translations into Greek and Latin Verse, *with Jebb's autograph inscription, ornamented cloth, uncut* *Cambridge,* 1873

639 Johnston (T. B.) and J. A. Robertson, Historical Geography of the Clans of Scotland, *coloured map and plans* *Edinb.* 1873

640 Juvenal's Satires translated with Notes by W. Gifford, *portrait, old calf* 1802

641 Kennett (Bp. W.) Parochial Antiquities, 2 vol. *portrait and plates, uncut* *Oxford,* 1818

642 Kitchin (G. W.) Life of Pope Pius II *Printed for Arundel Society,* 1881

643 Labre (B. Benedetto Giuseppe) Vita data in Luce in Occasione della sua Beatificazione, *portrait, Roma,* 1860

644 Layard (Sir A. H.) Six Accounts of Frescoes by Perugino, Nelli, Pinturicchio, G. Sanzio, Girlandaio, Masolino, Masaccio and Lippi, *printed for the Arundel Society,* 1856-68—Weale (W. H. J.) Hans Memling, *ib.* 1865, *half red morocco, top edge gilt* *in 1 vol.*

645 Lee (F. G.) Directorium Anglicanum, *plates, vellum,* 1865

646 Le Keux (J.) Memorials of Cambridge in a Series of Views with Descriptions by T. Wright and H. L. Jones, 2 vol. LARGE PAPER, *india proofs,* 1841-42— With C. H. Cooper's Account of Emmanuel College, *views, Cambridge,* 1861, *added*

647 Liddell (H. G.) and R. Scott, Greek-English Lexicon, *russia extra* *Oxford,* 1845

648 Lithographed Signatures of the Members of the British Association for the Advancement of Science who met at Cambridge, June 1833, with Report of Proceedings, *facsimiles, half gilt calf, uncut* *Cambridge,* 1833

649 Lockhart (J. G.) Ancient Spanish Ballads, *half red morocco* *Edinb.* 1823

650 London. Chronicles of the Mayors and Sheriffs (1188-1274), and French Chronicle of London translated by H. T. Riley, *with translator's autograph inscription,* 1863

651 London Liber Albus, compiled by J. Carpenter and Sir R. Whitington, translated by H. T. Riley, *autograph letter of translator added, uncut* 1861

652 Luard (H. R.) Catalogue of Manuscripts in Cambridge University Library, Index, *cloth, University arms in gold on sides* Cambridge, 1867

653 Luard (H. R.) Chronological List of The Graces, Documents and other Papers in the University Register which concern Cambridge University Library, LARGE PAPER *ib.* 1870

654 Luard (H. R.) Mathematical Papers, *Autograph MSS.* (3)

655 Lysons (D. and S.) Cambridgeshire, *plates, half calf gilt* 1810

FOLIO.

656 Doré (G.) Le Juif errant, *music and* 12 *plates, Paris,* 1862

657 Du Bartas (G. S.) His Divine Weekes and Workes with a Compleate Collection of all the other most delightfull Workes translated and written by that famous Philomusus Joshua Sylvester, *engraved title by Elstrack, calf gilt* 1621

658 DUGDALE (SIR W.) BARONAGE OF ENGLAND, 3 vol. in 1, *pedigrees, fine copy in old gilt russia* 1675-76

659 Duranti (G.) Divinorum Officiorum Rationale, *Nurembergœ, A. Koburger,* 1481—Hemmerlini (Felicis) Opuscula et Tractatus, *s. l. & a. circa* 1480—Tritemii (J.) Sermones et Exhortationes in Monachos, *Argentinœ,* 1516 —Gesta Rhomanorum cum Applicationibus moralisatis ac misticis, *s. l.* 1488, *fine copies, book-plate with his portrait of P. Hypodemander,* 1586, *oak boards covered in stamped pigskin in* 1 *vol.*

660 Epinal Glossary, Latin and English of the Eighth Century Photo-lithographed from the original MS. by W. Griggs, and edited with Transliteration, Introduction and Notes by H. Sweet 1883

661 ETYMOLOGICUM MAGNUM, Græce, cura M. Musuri, FIRST EDITION, *old calf, Larcher's copy*
Venetüs, *Z. Calliergi,* 1499

*** Rare. The Roxburghe copy sold for £18 10s.

662 Facsimiles of Ancient Manuscripts in the British Museum and of one in the Bodleian Library in a Portfolio (19)

663 Farren (R.) Etchings to illustrate the Birds of Aristophanes, *plates* *Cambridge*, 1884
664 FLAXMAN (J.) CLASSICAL COMPOSITIONS FOR HOMER,
HESIOD AND ÆSCHYLUS, 4 vol. in 1, *fine impressions
of the outline engravings, green morocco extra, borders of
gold, gilt edges, by J. Wright* 1805-15-17-31
665 Flaxman (J.) Designs for Dante, 110 *outline engravings,
morocco extra, gilt edges* 1807
666 Gazæ (Theodori) Introductiva Grammatica et de Mensibus
Opusculum ; Apollonius de Constructione; et Herodianus
de Metris. Omnia Græce, FIRST EDITION, *old calf*
Venetiis, Aldus, 1495

₊ Scarce. Sir M. Sykes's copy sold for £6 10s.

667 Germanicarum Rerum Scriptores ex Bibliotheca M. Fre-
heri curante B. G. Struvio, 3 vol. *vol. III slightly
wormed, vellum* *Argentorati*, 1717
668 Germanicarum Rerum Scriptores aliquot insignes qui
Historiam Germanorum a Carolo Magno ad Carolum V
usque per Annales Litteris consignarunt Collectore J.
Pistorio, 3 vol. *fine copy in stamped pigskin, with clasps*
Ratisponæ, 1731
669 Gozzini (V.) Monumenti Sepolcrali della Toscana, 48
engravings by P. Lasinio, half russia, top edge gilt
Firenze, 1819
670 GUILLIM (J.) DISPLAY OF HERALDRY, BEST EDITION,
*portraits, the numerous coats of arms correctly coloured,
fine copy in red morocco extra, gilt edges, by Hayday*, 1724
671 Hardy (Sir T. D.) Report on the Athanasian Creed in
Connexion with the Utrecht MS. Psalter, and Further
Report on the Utrecht Psalter, *facsimiles, autograph
letters of Sir T. D. Hardy added*, 2 vol. *half calf gilt*
1872-74
672 Herodotus, Græce, FIRST EDITION, *Bp. Blomfield's copy
with his book-plate, old russia* *Venetiis, Aldus*, 1502
673 HESIODI OPERA, Gr. et Lat. cum Notis Variorum edidit
T. Robinson, LARGEST PAPER (only 10 copies printed),
*bust of Hesiod, and plate, fine copy in old English red
morocco, borders of gold, gilt edges* *Oxonii*, 1737

₊ The rarest of all the Classics printed at the Sheldon
Press. The Duke of Grafton's copy sold for £105.

674 Hesychii Lexicon, Græce, cum Notis Variorum et J.
Alberti, 2 vol. LARGE PAPER, *portrait of Alberti, old
russia* *Lugd. Bat.* 1746-66
675 Hill (Sir. J.) British Herbal, *numerous plates* 1756
676 Hodgkin (J.) Calligraphia Græca et Pœcilographia Græca,
engraved throughout 1794

677 Holbein (Jean) Œuvre et Vie, par C. de Mechel, part I
Triomphe de la Mort, 48 *cuts and 2 plates of Triumphs
of Poverty and Riches ;* Part II, Passion de Notre-
Seigneur, 12 *plates*; Part III, Costumes Suisses du
XVI⁶ Siècle, 12 *plates ;* Part IV, XII Portraits
d'Hommes illustres du XVI⁶ Siècle (Family of Sir T.
More, Holbein's Wife and Child, J. Meier and Wife,
Froben, Holbein, Amerbach, Venus and Cupid, Lais,
Sir T. More and outline Engraving of his Family), *half
red morocco, uncut* Basle, 1780
678 HOMERI OPERA, Græce, 2 vol. *vol. I very large, ruled,
vol. II shorter, blue morocco extra, gilt edges, by Zaehnsdorf Florentiæ, Sumptibus B. et N. Nerliorum,* 1488
** The first edition of Homer must always be considered
the foundation of a collection of classics, but owing to
most copies having been secured for public libraries, its
occurrence at sales is so extremely rare that an opportunity
for purchase, once neglected, may not occur again in a
century. Dr. Hawtrey's copy sold for £85, and Sir J.
Thorold's for the same sum.
679 Homeri Interpres pervetustus (Scholia Græca in Iliadem)
FIRST EDITION *of the Scholia afterwards published with
name of Didymus as the author, old calf, rare, Romæ,* 1517
680 Homeri Iliados Picturæ antiquæ ex Codice Mediolanensi
Bibliothecæ Ambrosianæ, 59 *facsimiles, Romæ,* 1835—
Virgilii Picturæ antiquæ ex Codicibus Vaticanis, 72
facsimiles, ib. 1835, *half calf gilt in 1 vol.*
681 Jacobi Magni de Parisius Zophilogium, *fine copy in red
morocco, gilt edges, by Derome*
s. l. & a. sed Coloniæ circa 1471
** Supposed by Hain (10472) to have been printed at
Cologne.
682 Josephi (Flavii) Opera, Græce, Cura Arnoldi Peraxyli
Ablenii, FIRST EDITION, *fine copy in red morocco extra,
gilt edges Basileæ,* 1544
683 Jovii (P.) Elogia Virorum Literis illustrium, *woodcut
portraits* (including Sir T. More and Bp. Fisher), *half
red morocco ib.* 1577
684 JULII POLLUCIS ONOMASTICUM, Gr. et Lat. cum Notis
Variorum curantibus J. H. Lederlino et T. Hemsterhuis,
2 vol. LARGE PAPER, *frontispiece and arms of Amsterdam,
fine copy in pigskin, gilt edges, by Padeloup,* Amst. 1706
** Scarce. This copy sold for £6 10s. in Watson Taylor's
sale.
685 Justini Martyris (S.) Opera, Græce, FIRST EDITION, *autograph of "* Jo. Alberti Fabricii," *fine copy in old red
morocco, richly ornamented with gold tooling, gilt edges*
Lutetiæ, R. Stephanus, 1551

686 Letts's Popular County Atlas, 12 *parts, coloured maps, n.d.*

687 Lycophronis Alexandra cum Is. Tzetzis Scholiis Græce. Adjectus est Joannis Tzetzæ Historiarum Liber Versibus politicis Græce conscriptus et a P. Lacisio Latine conversus, 2 vol. in 1, FIRST SEPARATE EDITION, *wormed, old stamped calf* Basileæ, 1546

688 Lycophronis Alexandra Gr. et Lat. cum Græcis Is. Tzetzis Commentariis et Notis Variorum cura J. Potteri, LARGE PAPER, *old English red morocco, gilt edges* Oxonii, 1697

689 Lycophronis Alexandra Gr. et Lat. cum Tzetzæ Scholiis Græcis et Commentariis Cura J. Potteri, LARGE PAPER, *frontispiece, old calf* ib. 1702

690 Magni (Olai, *Archiepiscopi Upsalensis*) Historia de Gentibus Septentrionalibus, *numerous woodcuts, morocco extra, gilt edges* Romæ, 1555

  *** This edition has become famous by Sir W. Scott in his Pirate, making it a favorite of the Udaller.

691 Mantuani (Baptistæ) Omnia Opera, *calf* Bononiæ, 1502

692 Matthæi Westmonasteriensis Flores Historiarum, FIRST EDITION 1567

693 Matthæi Westmonasteriensis Flores Historiarum præcipue de Rebus Britannicis, *oak boards covered in stamped leather* T. Marshius, 1570

694 Matthæi Westmonasteriensis Flores Historiarum, *calf extra, rough leaves, many uncut, top edge gilt, with various critiques added* ib. 1570

695 MATTHÆI PARIS HISTORIA MAJOR cum Rogeri Wendoveri, Willielmi Rishangeri Authorisque collata. Accesserunt Duorum Offarum Regum et XXIII Abbatum S. Albani Vitæ Editore W. Wats, 2 vol. LARGE PAPER, *titles to vol. II inlaid, portrait, blue morocco extra, gilt edges* 1640

  *** Very rare on large paper. Dent's copy sold for £13 13s.

696 Matthæus Paris. Another copy on small paper, 2 vol. (*vol. II wants titles), MS. notes by Dr. Luard, half vellum* 1640

THIRD DAY'S SALE.

OCTAVO ET INFRA.

LOT

697 Index Librorum prohibitorum, *with MS. additions and various Decreta* (1838-48) *added, vellum,* Romæ, 1835

698 Ingleby (C. M.) Complete View of the Shakspere Controversy, *facsimiles, with author's autograph inscription* 1861

699 Innes (C.) Memoir of Prof. A. Dalzel, *portrait, half morocco, uncut, top edge gilt* Edinb. 1861

*** Privately printed for presents only.

700 Irving (J.) Annals of our Time, *half morocco* 1871

701 Irving (Washington) Tales of the Alhambra ; Legends of the Conquest of Spain ; and Conquest of Granada, 1851 —Lives of Mahomet and his Successors, 1850— Chronicle of the Conquest of Granada, 2 vol. *half calf extra, Paris,* 1829—Sketch Book, *portrait, half calf extra, Leipzig,* 1843 — Knickerbocker's History of New York, 1850—Voyages of Columbus, 1837 (7)

702 Isocratis Orationes et Epistolæ, Græce, *vellum* Venetiis, 1549

703 Jodrell (Sir R. P.) Illustrations of Euripides, 3 vol. *half russia* 1781-89

704 Jameson (Mrs.) Legends of the Monastic Orders as represented in the Fine Arts, *plates* 1852

705 Jameson (Mrs.) History of Our Lord as exemplified in Works of Art continued and completed by Lady Eastlake, 2 vol. *numerous illustrations* 1865

706 Jauffry, the Knight and the fair Brunissende, 20 *engravings by G. Doré, cloth, gilt edges* 1856

707 Jebb (R. C.) The Attic Orators from Antiphon to Isæos, 2 vol. *cloth, uncut, autograph letter of author added,* 1876

708 Jebb (R. C.) Introduction to Homer, *Glasgow,* 1887— Fitzgerald (E.) Euphranor, 1851—Harris (E. F. S) From Oxford to Rome, *frontispiece,* 1847 — Œhlenschlæger (A.) Axel and Valborg, with other Poems translated by P. Butler, 1874—D'Ewes (Sir S.) College Life in the Time of James I, 1851 (4)

709 Jefferies (R.) Hodge and his Masters, 2 vol. FIRST EDITION 1880

710 Jefferies (R.) Field and Hedgerow 1889

711 Johnstone (J.) Life of Dr. S. Parr, 2 vol. LARGE PAPER,
 3 *portraits* 1829
712 Joinville (J. de) Histoire de Saint Louis, Credo et Lettre
 à Louis X. Texte original accompagné d'une Traduction par Natalis de Wailly, *illuminated facsimile and
 vignettes, half red morocco* Paris, 1874
713 Jones (J. W.) List of Books of Reference in the Reading
 Room of the British Museum, *plans* 1859
714 Journal of Classical and Sacred Philology, 4 vol. *half calf
 gilt* Cambridge, 1854-59
715 Journal of Philology, edited by W. G. Clark, J. E. Mayor,
 W. A. Wright, I. Bywater, and H. Jackson, 18 vol.
 half calf gilt, Cambridge, 1868-90 ; and Nos. 37 and 38,
 unbound, ib. 1891 (20)
716 Junius, edited by G. Woodfall, 3 vol. *facsimiles, calf extra*
 1814
717 Justinus et Æmylius Probus, *vellum, Venetiis, Aldus,* 1522
718 Juvenalis Satyræ, with a Commentary by J. E. B. Mayor,
 2 vol. in 3 Cambridge, 1869-78
719 Juvenalis Satyræ, with a Commentary by J. E. B. Mayor,
 2 vol. *cloth, uncut* 1886 and 1881
720 Keble (J.) Christian Year, *autograph letters of Keble and
 W. G. Clark added, morocco extra, gilt red edges*
 Oxford, 1849
721 Keble (J.) Christian Year, *morocco, gilt edges, Oxford,*
 1845 — Hymnary, *n. d.*—Book of Common Prayer,
 Oxford, 1860—Martyrs and Saints of the first Twelve
 Centuries, 1887 ; and 16 others, Religious (20)
722 Keller (G.) Leute von Seldwyla, 2 vol. in 1, *ornamented
 cloth, Berlin,* 1885—Rückert (F.) Œstliche Rosen,
 vignettes, half morocco, gilt edges, Leipzig, 1822—Hahn-
 Hahn (Ida Gräfin) Gräfin Faustine, *half calf gilt,
 Berlin,* 1841—Gands (P.) Guide to German Literature,
 Frankfort, 1841—Ollendorff (H. G.) German Grammar,
 ib. 1846—Tiarks (J. G.) German Grammar, 1845 (6)
723 Ken (Bp. T.) Prose Works, *calf extra* 1838
724 King (Dr. W.) Original Works in Verse and Prose, 3 vol.
 old calf gilt 1776
725 Kingsley (C.) Poems, 1878—At Last, a Christmas in the
 West Indies, 2 vol. *illustrations,* 1871 (3)
726 Kingsley (C.) The Heroes, or Greek Fairy Tales, *plates,*
 1879 — McPherson (J. G.) Fairy Tales of Science,
 Edinb. 1889 — Mallock (W. H.) New Paul and Virginia,
 n. d.—Mayo (H.) Letters on Truths in Popular Super-
 stitions, 1849 (4)
727 Kington (T. L.) History of Frederick II, Emperor of the
 Romans, 2 vol. *half calf gilt* 1862

728 Kirton (J. W.) True Royalty (Life of Queen Victoria), *portraits of the Queen and illustrations* 1880

729 Knight (S.) Life of Dean J. Colet, *portrait and plates Oxford,* 1823

730 Knight (S.) Life of Dean J. Colet, LARGE PAPER, *portrait and plates, half blue morocco extra, uncut, top edge gilt ib.* 1823

731 Lady's Guide to her Household and Dinner Table, 1861— Teacher's Manual, 1879 ; and others *a parcel*

732 Lamartine (A. de) Voyage en Orient, 2 vol. *stained, Paris,* 1849—Histoire de la Révolution de 1848, 2 vol. *Bruxelles,* 1849, *half calf gilt* 4 *vol.*

733 Lamb (C.) Essays of Elia and Last Essays, 2 vol. *frontispieces, blue morocco extra, uncut, top edges gilt* 1888

734 La Motte Fouqué (Baron de) Sintram and his Companions (translated by Julius Hare), *red morocco, gilt edges, very rare* 1820

735 Landon (E. H.) Manual of Councils of the Holy Catholick Church, *half calf gilt,* 1846—Ffoulkes (E. S.) Christendom's Divisions in East and West, 2 vol. 1865-67 (3)

736 Lanzi (L.) Storia Pittorica della Italia, 6 vol. *Pisa,* 1815-17—Boni (O.) Elogio dell' Abate L. Lanzi, *ib.* 1816, *vellum* 7 *vol.*

737 Lappenberg (J. M.) History of England under the Anglo-Saxon Kings, translated by B. Thorpe, 2 vol. *scarce,* 1845

738 Lappenberg (J. M.) History of England under the Norman Kings, translated by B. Thorpe *Oxford,* 1857

739 Latin-Anglo-Saxon Glossary of VIIIth Century, edited by J. H. Hessels, *editor's autograph inscription Cambridge,* 1890

740 Lauder (W.) Essay on Milton's Use and Imitation of the Moderns in his Paradise Lost 1750

741 Leadam (T. R.) Homœopathy as applied to the Diseases of Females, 1857—Baret (W.) Applied Homœopathy, 1871—Guernsey (E.) Homœopathic Domestic Practice, 1864—Hirschel (B.) Guide du Medecin Homœopathe, *Paris,* 1858—Liberali (C.) Hygienic-Medical Hand-Book, *Rome,* 1878—Mattei (Count C.) Electro-Homœopathy, *portrait, Bologna,* 1880—Hunter (G. M.) Hunterian Oration, *Camb.* 1879—Latham (P. W.) Harveian Oration, *ib.* 1888 ; and 4 others, Medical (13)

742 Leigh (Medora) History and Autobiography, edited by C. Mackay, 1869 — Stowe (Mrs. H. B.) History of the Byron Controversy, 1870—Stowe-Byron Controversy, *n. d.* (3)

743 Leighton (Archbp. R.) Works   1839

744 Leighton (J.) Paris under the Commune, *plates*, 1871—
Yonge (C. M.) Cameos from English History, 1874—
Maunder (S.) Treasury of Knowledge, 1843 ; and 10
others   (13)

745 Lelandus (J.) de Scriptoribus Britannicis, 2 vol. in 1, *calf*
Oxonii, 1709

746 Le Neve (J.) Fasti Ecclesiæ Anglicanæ, from the earliest
Time to 1715, with Continuation to the present Time,
by Sir T. D. Hardy, 3 vol. *calf gilt*   *Oxford*, 1854

747 Leo the Great (Saint) Eighteen Sermons on the Incarna-
tion, translated, with Notes, by W. Bright, *autograph*
letter of translator added   1862

748 Leonetti (A.) Papa Alessandro VI, 3 vol. *Bologna*, 1880
—Tabarrini (M.) Studj di Critica storica, *Firenze*, 1876
—Rufini (A.) Dizionario delle Strade, Piazze, Borghi
e Vicoli di Roma, *Roma*, 1847, *half gilt vellum*   5 *vol.*

749 Lesage (A. R.) Gil Blas, *portrait, half calf gilt, Paris*,
1857—Gasparin (Comte A. de) La Famille, 2 vol. *ib.*
1873—Ohnet (G.) Volonté, *ib.* 1888—Ordinaire (D.)
Dictionnaire de Mythologie, *ib. s. d.*; and 10 others,
French   (15)

750 Letters written by eminent Persons in the XVII and
XVIIIth Centuries : to which are added Hearne's
Journeys to Reading and to Whaddon Hall, and Lives
of eminent Men by J. Aubrey, 2 vol. in 3, *half calf*,
uncut   1813

751 Lewis (M. G.) Tales of Wonder, 2 vol. LARGE PAPER, *tree-*
marbled calf extra, uncut, top edges gilt, by Wilson, 1801

752 Leyseri (P.) Historia Poetarum et Poematum medii Ævi,
half green morocco, gilt edges   *Halœ*, 1721

753 Library (The), a Magazine of Bibliography and Literature,
edited by J. Y. W. MacAlister, *vol. I cloth, and No.* 13
to 28 *inclusive sewed*   1889-91

754 Libri (G.) Catalogue of his Manuscripts, with English and
French Introduction (by John H. Bohn and G. Libri),
facsimiles   1859

755 Liddell and Scott's Abridged Greek-English Lexicon,
Oxford, 1858—Riddle (J. E.) English-Latin Dictionary,
1840—Crombie (A.) Gymnasium, 1836—Holden (H. A.)
Foliorum Silvula, part I, *Camb.* 1862—Gillespie (G. K.)
Formative Greek Grammar, *author's autograph letter*,
1842—Schinas (M.) Grammaire du Grec moderne, *Paris*,
1829 ; and 4 others   (10)

756 Liddon (H. P.) Bampton Lectures, *autograph letter of*
author added   1868

757 Life of Lavinia Beswick, alias Fenton, alias Polly Peacham, *margin of last leaf mended, scarce* 1728

758 Liebermann (F.) Ungedruckte Anglo-Normanische Geschichtsquellen, *half vellum* *Strassburg*, 1879

*** Containing 17 important documents, one in Anglo-Saxon and the rest in Latin.

759 Lightfoot (Bp. J. B.) St. Paul's Epistles to Galatians, Philippians, Colossians and Philemon. A revised Text, with Introductions, Notes and Dissertations, 3 vol.
1865-68-75

760 Lightfoot (Bp. J. B.) Essays on the Work entitled Supernatural Religion 1889

761 Liturgia Armena ed in Italiano per Cura del P. Gabriele Avedichian Mechitarista, *plates* *Venezia*, 1854

762 Liturgiæ Britannicæ, with Church of Scotland Liturgy arranged to shew their Variations, by W. Keeling, 1851

763 Lives of J. Leland, T. Hearne and Anthony à Wood (edited by T. Warton and W. Huddesford), 2 vol. LARGE PAPER, *portraits, calf* *Oxford*, 1772

764 Lobley (J. A.) The Church and the Churches in Southern India *Cambridge*, 1870

765 Lobo (J.) Voyage to Abyssinia, with Continuation by M. Legrand, translated by Dr. S. Johnson, *calf extra*, 1735

766 Lockhart (J. G.) Life of Sir Walter Scott *Edinb.* 1845

767 Longini Opera, Gr. et Lat. cum Notis J. Toupii, *red morocco* *Oxonii*, 1778

768 Longus, Daphnis and Chloe, translated by Angel Day, *reprint of the unique original*, edited by J. Jacobs, *vellum* 1890

769 Lowndes (W. T.) Bibliographer's Manual of English Literature, enlarged by H. G. Bohn, 6 vol. *half calf gilt* 1864

770 Loyolæ (S. Ignatii) Exercitia Spiritualia, *vellum* *Romæ*, 1615

771 Luard (H. R.) Lives of Edward the Confessor, *MS. notes by Dr. Luard, half calf gilt* 1858

*** Containing Estoire de S. Aedward, in Norman-French verse, with Glossary ; Vita B. Edvardi et Vita Æduardi Regis.

772 Luard (H. R.) Catalogue of Adversaria and printed Books containing MS. Notes preserved in Cambridge University Library, *half green morocco, uncut, top edge gilt* *Camb.* 1864

773 Luard (H. R.) Graduati Cantabrigienses (300-1872), *with account for sale of the work added* *Cantab.* 1873

774 Luard (H. R.) on the Relations between England and
Rome during the earlier Portion of the Reign of
Henry III, 65 *copies*   *Cambridge*, 1877

775 Luard (H. R.) Chronological List of Documents in Cam-
bridge University Registry, *Cambridge*, 1870—Sinker
(R.) Catalogue of XVth Century Books, and of English
Books printed before 1601, in Trinity College Library,
autograph letter of author added, *ib*. 1876-85—Schiller-
Szinessy (S. M.) Catalogue of Hebrew Manuscripts in
Cambridge University Library, *ib*. 1876   (4)

776 Luard (H. R.) List of Documents in the University
Registry (1266-1544), 12 *copies*, 1876—Suggestions on
Election of Council, Duties of Vice-Chancellor and His-
torical Tripos, 5 *copies*, 1866—Remarks on New Statutes,
3 *copies*, 1858—On the Relations between England and
Rome, temp. Henry III, 1877—On the proposed Title
A. C. 5 *copies*, 1860—Remarks on Bursar's Proposal,
printed for Fellows only, 1857—Preface to Newton Cata-
logue, 1888—Diary of E. Rud, 1860—Sermon at S.
Edwards' Church, 1872   (30)

778 Luciani Opera, Gr. et Lat. studiis Societatis Bipontinæ,
10 vol. *calf extra*   *Biponti*, 1789-93

779 Luckock (H. M.) The Bishops in the Tower, 1887—The
Intermediate State, 1890—Studies in the History of the
Book of Common Prayer, 1882   (3)

780 Lucretius de Rerum Natura, with English Translation and
Notes by H. A. J. Munro, 2 vol. *presentation copy, with
2 autograph letters from editor*   *Cambridge*, 1864

781 Lucretius, edente H. A. I. Munro, *Cantab*. 1860—Goffeaux
(D. J.) Robinson Crusoeus, 1823—Scioppii (G.) Infamia
Famiani, &c. *Soræ*, 1658; and 1 other   (4)

782 Lusus alteri Westmonasterienses quibus accedit Declama-
tionum quæ vocantur Epigrammatum Delectus curantibus J. Mure, H. Bull et C. B. Scott, 2 vol.
Oxonii, 1863-67
₊ Presentation copy from C. B. Scott, with his autograph
inscriptions.

783 Lyra Catholica (Breviary and Missal Hymns), translated
by E. Caswall, *blue morocco, gilt edges*   1849

784 Lyra Germanica, translated by Catherine Winkworth, *both
series*, 2 vol. *red morocco, gilt edges*   1859-60

785 Lytton (Lord) Pelham, 1854—Rienzi, Zanoni, Last Days
of Pompeii, Last of the Barons and Night and Morning,
6 vol. in 5, *half calf extra, Leipzig*, 1842-43   (6)

786 Macaulay (T. B. Lord) History of England from the
Accession of James II, 10 vol. *cloth*   *Leipzig*, 1849-61

787 Macaulay (T. B. Lord) Lays of Ancient Rome, 1844—
  Grotius (H.) Adamus Exul, translated by F. Barham,
  half calf gilt, 1839—Coleridge (Hartley) Poems, *half
  calf gilt, Leeds*, 1833—Rogers (S.) Poems and Italy,
  2 vol. in 1, *half calf gilt*, 1839-40—Dodd (W.) Thoughts
  in Prison, *portrait*, 1781— Keble (J.) Miscellaneous
  Poems, *Oxford*, 1869   (6)
788 Mac-Carthy Reagh (Comte de) Catalogue de sa Bibliothèque, 2 vol. *MS. Notes and prices, uncut, Paris*, 1815
789 McClintock (F. L.) Narrative of the Discovery of the Fate
  of Sir J. Franklin and his Companions, *maps and illustrations*   1859
790 McCrie (T.) Life of John Knox, *russia extra, gilt edges*
                                                Edinb. 1861
791 Macmillan's Magazine, vol. 22, 23 and 24, 1870-71—English Historical Review, No. 10 and 12, 1888—Murray's
  Magazine, No. 33, 1889 — Modern Review, No. 4, 1880
  —Book-Prices Current, part IV, 1890 — Archæological
  Journal, No. 74, 1862 — Christian Remembrancer, No.
  56, 1847—Palestine Pilgrims' Text Society, No. 1, An-
  toninus, 1884, and No. 3, Procopius, *autograph letter of
  W. Besant*, 1886—Revue Historique pour Septembre-
  Octobre, 1878, *Paris*, 1878   (13)
792 Macray (W. D.) Annals of the Bodleian Library   1868
793 Macray (W. D.) Manual of British Historians to A.D. 1600,
  W. Pickering, 1845 — Johnston (K.) Atlas of Modern
  Geography and Historical Atlas, 2 vol. *coloured maps,
  Edinb. n. d.*   (3)
794 Macrobii in Somnium Scipionis Explanatio et Saturnalia.
  Item Censorinus de Die natali, *wormed, sold with all
  faults*   *Venetiis, Aldus*, 1528
795 Maginn (W.) Homeric Ballads, 1850 — Akenside (M.)
  Poetical Works, with Life by Rev. A. Dyce, *portrait,
  W. Pickering*, 1835—Walker (W. S.) Poetical Remains,
  with Life by Rev. J. Moultrie, 1852 — Longfellow (H.
  W.) Poems, *Liverpool*, 1848—Beattie (J.) Minstrel, and
  other Poems, *portrait*, 1806 — Smyth (W.) English
  Lyrics, *half morocco*, 1815—Temple (N.) and E. Trevor,
  Tannhäuser, 1861 — Garth (Sir S.) Dispensary, with
  Key, 2 vol. in 1, *plates, calf*, 1741-46 — Prince (J. C.)
  Autumn Leaves, *Hyde*, 1856—Anstey (C.) Pleader's
  Guide, *half calf gilt*, 1808—Byron (Lord) Tales, 2 vol.
  vignette titles, 1837   (12)
796 Maine (Sir H. S.) Popular Government, *autograph letter of
  author added*   1886
797 Maitland (S. R.) Two Letters to Rose, with Strictures on
  Milner's Church History, 1835 — Letter to King, 1835
  —Remarks on King's Letter, 1836, *half russia, in 1 vol.*

798 Maitland (S. R.) Eruvin, 1850—Eight Essays, *frontis-piece*, 1852—Voluntary System, 1837—False Worship, 1856—Superstition and Science, 1855—Chatterton, 1857 —Letter to Mill, 1839—On Mesmerism, 1849—Six Letters on Fox's Martyrs, 1837 — On prophetic Period of Daniel and St. John, 1837—King (J.) Maitland not authorized to censure Milner, 1835—Maitland's Answer to King, 1835 (12)

799 Maitland (S. R.) List of early printed Books and of English Books printed before 1600, in Lambeth Archiepiscopal Library, 2 vol. 1843-45

*** Privately printed for presents only.

800 Malory (Sir T.) History of King Arthur and Knights of the Round Table, 3 vol. 1858

801 Man in the Moon, edited by A. Smith and A. B. Reach, 5 vol. *numerous humorous illustrations by Phiz, Kenny Meadows, Sala and other artists, half morocco* n. d.

802 Manning (C. R.) Monumental Brasses remaining in England, *interleaved, russia extra* 1846

803 Mansel (H. L.) Gnostic Heresies of the first and second centuries, edited by J. B. Lightfoot, *Editor's autograph inscription* 1875

804 Manutii (Paulli) Apophthegmata, *vellum* *Venetiis, Aldus*, 1577

805 Manzoni (A.) Opere Complete, *portrait and plates, calf extra* *Parigi*, 1843

806 Marco Polo's Book concerning the Kingdoms and Marvels of the East, translated and edited with Notes by Colonel Henry Yule, 2 vol. *maps and other illustrations, calf extra, gilt edges* 1871

807 Marsh (Bp. H.) Letters to Archdeacon Travis, *uncut, scarce* *Leipzig*, 1795

808 Marsh (Bp. H.) History of the Politicks of Great Britain and France, 2 vol. *old gilt calf* 1800

809 Marsh (Bp. H.) Memoir of the Rev. T. Jones, *privately printed, Cambridge*, 1808 — Whewell (W.) Sunday Thoughts, *very rare, ib. n. d.;* and other scarce Tracts in the Volume, *half calf extra*

810 Martin (M.) Voyage to St. Hilda, *plate*, 1753—Mistakes in Sir W. Dugdale's Baronage, 1730—Charles I, Eikon Basilike, *no portrait*, 1648—Davies (J.) Durham Cathedral, *with Horace Walpole's bookplate*, 1672 (4)

811 Maskell (W.) Ancient Liturgy of the Church of England according to the Uses of Sarum, Bangor, York and Hereford, and the modern Roman Liturgy arranged in parallel Columns *W. Pickering*, 1846

812 Mason (A. J.) Persecution of Diocletian, *with Author's autograph inscription* *Cambridge*, 1876

813 Mason (A. J.) Relation of Confirmation to Baptism as taught by the Western Fathers, 1890—Wheatly (C.) on the Book of Common Prayer, *frontispiece*, 1848— Spelman (Sir H.) History and Fate of Sacrilege, 1846 —Paley (W.) Moral and Political Philosophy, *portrait and vignette title*, 1822 (4)

814 Mason (P. H.) Letters on the supposed Cruelties of 2 Sam. xii. 31, *Cambridge*, 1887-89—Essay on Psalm LXVIII, *ib.* 1886—Sinker (P.) Psalm of Habakkuk, *ib.* 1890, *half calf gilt* *in* 1 *vol.*

815 Mathias (T. J.) Runic Odes from the Norse, 1790—Poesie Liriche Toscane, *Napoli*, 1818—Odes English and Latin, *Not published*, 1798; and a Collection of 13 Tracts (*several very rare*) *by Mathias, with his autograph, in* 1 *vol.* (4)

816 Mattei (Comte C.) Médicine électro-homéopathique, *portrait, Nice*, 1883—Chapmell (E. C.) Domestic Homœopathy, 1859—Rudock (E. H.) Homœopathic Treatment of Children, 1874 (3)

817 Matthew Paris's English History, translated by J. A. Giles, 3 vol. *portrait* 1852-54

818 Maundrell (H.) Journey from Aleppo to Jerusalem with Journal from Grand Cairo to Mount Sinai, translated by Bp. R. Clayton, LARGE PAPER, *plates, russia extra, leather joints, gilt edges* 1810

819 Maundevile (Sir John) Voiage and Travaile treating of the Way to Hierusalem and of Marvayles of Inde and other Countryes, with Notes and Glossary by J. O. Halliwell-Phillipps, *woodcuts, half calf extra, uncut, t. e. g.* 1883

820 Maurice (C. E.) Stephen Langton, 1872—Macgregor (Cecilia) St. Edward the Confessor, 1873—Fullerton (Lady G.) St. Frances of Rome, 1855—Perry (G. G.) Bp. R. Grosseteste, *plates*, 1871—Bedford (H.) St. Vincent de Paul, *portrait*, 1856—Cox (G. W.) St. Boniface, 1853—Faber (F. W.) St. Philip Neri, 1850 (6)

821 Maurice (F. D.) Eustace Conway, 3 vol. FIRST EDITION, *half red morocco, scarce* 1834

822 Maurice (F. D.) Friendship of Books and other Lectures 1874

823 Maurice (F. D.) Sermons in Country Churches, 1873— Gospel and Epistles of St. John, 2 vol. 1867—Stephen (Caroline E.) Service of the Poor, *autograph of F. D. Maurice*, 1871 (4)

824 Maurice (F. D.) Social Morality, *Camb.* 1869—The Conscience, *ib.* 1860—Moral and Metaphysical Philosophy, 2 vol. 1872, *presentation copies with author's autograph inscriptions, cloth, uncut* 4 *vol.*

825 Maurice (F. D.) Life edited by his Son, 2 vol. *portraits,*
with Gladstone Letter added 1884
826 Maxwell (W. H.) Life of the Duke of Wellington, 3 vol.
LARGE PAPER, *portraits, maps, plans, views, &c. calf*
extra 1839-41
827 Maxwell (W. H.) Fortune of Hector O'Halloran, FIRST
EDITION, *plates by J. Leech, original cloth* 1846
828 Maxwell (W. H.) History of the Irish Rebellion in 1798,
with Memoirs of the Union and Emmett's Insurrection
in 1803, *portraits, and illustrations by G. Cruikshank,*
tree-marbled calf extra, uncut, top edge gilt 1852
829 Mayhew (H.) London Labour and London Poor, 4 vol.
portrait and numerous illustrations, half red morocco
extra 1851-62
830 Mayo (C.) Sermons on the Lord's Supper with Lecture on
Pestalozzi and other Papers, in 1 vol. *half morocco,*
1840-56—Krause (W. H.) Sermons, vol. II and III,
edited by C. S. Stanford, *Dublin,* 1853-55—Carter (T. T.)
Lent Lectures, 1860—Shirley (W. W.) Catalogue of
Wyclif's Works, *Oxford,* 1865; and 4 others, Religious (9)
831 Mayor (J. E. B.) The Latin Heptateuch, published piece-
meal, critically reviewed, 1889—Exercises on Latin Acci-
dence, *Camb.* 1871 (2)
832 Mayor (J. E. B.) Bibliographical Clue to Latin Literature, *Camb.* 1873—Cicero's Second Philippic, *ib.* 1861
—Edition of R. Ascham's Scholemaster, 1863—Bedæ
Historiæ Ecclesiasticæ Libri III et IV, *Camb.* 1878—
Homer's Odysseus in Greek with Commentary, 1873—
Letters of Archbp. Williams, &c. *only 50 copies printed,*
n. d. — Pliny's Letters, Book III, *Camb.* 1880 —
Quintiliani Institutonis Oratoriæ Liber, *ib.* 1872 (8)
833 Meadows (F. C.) Spanish and English Dictionary, 1860;
and 5 other French and Italian Dictionaries (6)
834 Melvill (H.) Sermons, 2 vol. 1845
835 Mendes da Costa (E.) Elements of Conchology, *plates,*
1776—Brown (T.) Conchologist's Text-Book, *plates,*
Glasgow, 1833—Woodward (S. P.) Manual of the
Mollusca, with Supplement, *numerous illustrations,*
1851-56 (4)
836 Michaelis (J. D.) Introduction to the New Testament,
translated by Bp. H. Marsh, 6 vol. *old calf extra* 1802
837 Michaud (J. F.) History of the Crusades, 3 vol. *maps,* 1852
838 Mill (J. S.) Autobiography, 1874—Evelyn (J.) Life of
Mrs. Godolphin, FIRST EDITION, *portrait,* 1847—Brewer
(T.) Memoirs of T. Carpenter, Town Clerk of London
in the Reigns of Henry V & VI, *view of City of London*
School, 1836 (3)

839 Mill (W. H.) University Sermons and Observations on the attempted Application of Pantheistic Principles to Criticism of the Gospels, 3 vol. *half red morocco ;* and 5 Single Sermons and Tracts by Mill, *Camb.* 1844-45-61 (8)

840 Milner (Dean I.) Life, Correspondence and unpublished Writings by his Niece Mary Milner, *portrait* 1842

841 Milman (Dean H. H.) History of Latin Christianity, 9 vol. *autograph letter of author added* 1864

842 Milman (Dean H. H.) History of the Jews, 3 vol. 1866

843 Milnes (R. M. *Lord Houghton*) Poems, *presentation copy with author's autograph inscription, calf extra, g. e.* 1838

844 Milton (J.) Paradise Lost, compared and revised by J. Hawkey, THICK PAPER, *reprinted title, old red morocco, richly ornamented with gold tooling, g. e. Dublin,* 1747

845 Milton (J.) Paradise Regained, and other Poetical Works, THICK PAPER, *blue morocco extra, uncut, top edge gilt*
Dublin, 1752

846 Milton (J.) Poetical Works, 1837—Homer's Iliad by A. Pope, *morocco, gilt edges, n. d.*—Homer's Odyssey by A. Pope, 2 vol. *calf extra, Chiswick,* 1820—Virgil by J. Dryden, *calf extra,* 1808 (5)

847 Miscellaneous Books 2 *parcels*

848 Missale ad Usum Sarum, Pars prima ; Temporale
Burntisland, 1861

849 Mitchell (T.) Index Græcitatis Platonicæ, 2 vol.
Oxonii, 1832

850 Moliere (J. B.) Œuvres, 6 vol. *calf* *Paris,* 1816

851 Montalembert (Comte de) Histoire de Sainte Elizabeth de Hongrie, 2 vol. *half calf gilt* *ib.* 1859

852 Montesquieu (C. Baron de) Œuvres complètes, 5 vol. *portrait, half calf gilt* *ib.* 1820

853 Moore (T.) Epistles, Odes and other Poems, 2 vol. *frontispiece, blue morocco, gilt edges,* 1807—Montgomery (J.) Wanderer of Switzerland and World before the Flood, with other Pieces, 2 vol. *panelled calf extra,* 1811-15—Thomson (J.) Seasons and Castle of Indolence, *frontispiece and vignette title, calf gilt,* 1816 — Keats (J.) Poetical Works, *portrait, cloth,* 1854—The Afterglow, 1867—Trench (Archbp. R. C.) Story of Justin Martyr and other Poems, 1857—Blanche Lisle and other Poems by Cecil Home (Angusta Davis), *Camb.* 1860 (9)

854 Morris (W.) Earthly Paradise, a Poem, 4 vol. 1871

855 Moss (J. W.) Manual of Classical Bibliography completed to end of 1836 by a Supplement, 2 vol. *half russia extra* 1837

856 Morley (H.) English Writers before Chaucer 1864

857 Morley (H.) How to make Home unhealthy, 1850—Lowell
(J. R.) Biglow Papers, 1862—Maurice (F. D.) Moral
Philosophy and Theology, 1866—Littledale (R. F.)
Innovations, *Oxford*, 1868—Pullen's Fight in Dame
Europa's School, 1870—Chesney (G.) Battle of Dork-
ing, *Edinb.* 1871—Williams (G.) Life of Bp. T.
Bellyngton, *Wells*, 1863, *half calf gilt*   *in* 1 *vol.*

858 Mullinger (J. Bass) History of Cambridge University,
3 vol. *autograph letter of author added*, 1873-1884-1888

859 Mullinger (J. B.) Cambridge University from 1535 to Accession of Charles I, *author's autograph inscription and
holograph letter of M. Creighton*   *Cambridge,* 1884

860 Munro (H. A. J.) Criticism and Elucidations of Catullus,
Camb. 1878—Virgilii Ætna revised, emended and ex-
plained by H. A. J. Munro, *ib.* 1867—Apuleius de Deo
Socratis cum Notis T. A. G. Buckley, 1844   (3)

861 Mure (W.) Tour in Greece and the Ionian Islands, 2 vol.
maps and plates   *Edinb.* 1842

862 Murray's Handbooks for Switzerland, Savoy, Piedmont,
Rome and Italy, 4 vol. *maps*, 1874-75—Baedeker's
Belgium, Holland and the Rhine, 2 vol. *maps and plans*,
1882-85; and various Maps and Plans   *a parcel*

863 Museum Criticum or Cambridge Classical Researches,
2 vol.   *Cambridge*, 1826

864 Museum Criticum or Cambridge Classical Researches,
edited by Bp. J. H. Monk, 2 vol. *cloth autograph letter
of Bp. Monk added, Cambridge*, 1826—Philological Museum, 2 vol. *ib.* 1832-33, *tree-marbled calf extra*,   4 *vol.*

865 Musgrave (S.) Dissertations on Grecian Mythology and
Chronology of Olympiads, LARGE PAPER, *half calf
gilt*   1782

866 Netherclift (F. G.) Hand-Book of Autographs, *numerous
facsimiles, morocco extra, gilt edges*   1862

867 Newman (J. H. Cardinal) Lectures on Justification, *calf
gilt*   1838

868 Newman (J. H. Cardinal) Lives of the English Saints,
15 vol. in 5, *half red morocco*   1844-45

869 Newman (J. H. Cardinal) Essay on the Development of
Christian Doctrine, *calf gilt*   1845

870 Newman (J. H. Cardinal) Lectures on the present Pos-
ition of Catholics in England, *calf gilt*   1851

871 Newman (J. H. Cardinal) Arians of the fourth Century,
Literally reprinted from the first Edition, *calf gilt*, 1854

872 Newman (J. H. Cardinal) Church of the Fathers, 1842—
Loss and Gain, 1858—Callista, 1856   (3)

873 Newman (J. H. Cardinal) Parochial and Plain Sermons,
8 vol. 1868—Sermons on Subjects of the Day, 1869,
cloth, uncut   9 *vol.*

874 Newton (Sir I.) Correspondence with Professor Cotes, including Letters of other eminent Men, *portrait*
Cambridge, 1850

875 Nibby (A.) Viaggio antiquario ne Contorni di Roma, 2 vol. *maps, plans and plates, Roma,* 1819—Del Foro Romano, della Via Sacra, dell' Anfiteatro Flavio e de' Luoghi adjacenti, *plates, ib.* 1819—Le Mura di Roma disegnate da Sir W. Gell illustrate con Testo e Note da A. Nibby, *plates, ib.* 1820, 4 vol. *vellum ;* and 2 others (6)

876 NICHOLS (J.) LITERARY ANECDOTES OF THE XVIIITH CENTURY, with Index, 9 vol. *portraits and plates, calf gilt,* 1812-16—ILLUSTRATIONS OF THE LITERARY HISTORY OF THE XVIIITH CENTURY, by J. and J. B. Nichols, 8 vol. *portraits and plates, half green morocco, uncut, top edges gilt,* 1817-58 17 *vol.*

877 Nicolas (Sir N. H.) Historic Peerage of England, continued by W. Courthope, *half red morocco,* 1857—Dod's Peerage, Baronetage and Knightage, 1883 (2)

878 North (Hon. Roger) Lives of Francis North, Baron Guilford, Hon. Sir Dudley North and Hon. and Rev. Dr. John North, 3 vol. *portrait, tree-marbled calf extra, uncut, top edges gilt, by Wilson* 1826

879 Officia Propria Passionis et Maternitatis ac Puritatis B. Mariæ Virginis, *red morocco, gilt edges, with bishop's arms in gold on sides* *Romœ,* 1832

880 Olivieri (L. P.) Il Senato Romano, *portraits, half gilt vellum, uncut* *Roma,* 1840

881 O'Meara (Barry E.) Napoleon in Exile, 2 vol. *portraits and view, green morocco extra, richly ornamented with bees and eagle stamped in gold on sides* 1822

882 Oppianus de Piscibus et de Venatione, Græce. Oppianus de Piscibus L. Lippio Interprete, *Venetiis, Aldus,* 1517 — Artemidorus de Somniorum Interpretatione et Synesius de Insomniis, Græce, FIRST EDITION, *ib.* 1518, *old panelled calf* *in* 1 *vol.*

  *** Sir J. Thorold's copy of Oppian sold for £3 3s. and his Artemidorus for £1 4s.

883 ORATORES ATTICI Græce ex Recensione Im. Bekkeri cum Indicibus Græcitatis a T. Mitchell, 10 vol. LARGE PAPER, *calf extra* *Oxon.* 1822-28

  *** Only 50 copies printed, each for £16 10s. unbound.

884 Oderici Vitalis Historia Ecclesiastica. Accedunt Anastasii IV et Adriani IV Epistolæ et Privilegia ; necnon Theobaldi Cantuariensis Archiepiscopi, Attonis aliorumque Opuscula, &c. accurante J. P. Migne *Paris,* 1855

F

885 Oxford Historical Society's Publications, vol. I to XIII
(*wanting IX and XII*) *Oxford*, 1885-89
886 Palæphatus de Incredibilibus, Gr. et Lat. cum Notis C.
Tollii *Amst. L. Elzevir*, 1649
887 Paley (W.) Natural Theology, 1811—Evidences of Christianity, 1819—Life, by G. W. Meadley, *portrait, Edinb.*
1810 (3)
888 Palgrave (Sir F.) Merchant and Friar, *frontispiece, half
calf gilt*, 1837—Etoniana, *Edinb.* 1865—Gairdner (J.)
Houses of Lancaster and York, 5 *maps*, 1874—Reeve
(H.) Petrarch, *Edinb.* 1878—Dyce (A.) Recollections
of Rogers, 1859—Pompeii, 2 vol. *woodcuts*, 1831-32 ;
and 8 others (15)
889 Pamphlets (Antiquarian), in 2 vol. *half calf gilt* (35)
890 Pamphlets (Miscellaneous), in 7 vol. *several privately
printed and scarce, half calf gilt* 1841-87
891 Pamphlets on the Irish Church and Ely, *half calf gilt*
1868-70
892 Parker (J. H.) Glossary of Architecture, 2 vol. in 3, *numerous plates and woodcuts, cloth, uncut* *Oxford*, 1850
893 Paræmiographi Græci edente T. Gaisford, *half russia*
Oxonii, 1836
894 Parr (S.) Præfatio ad Bellendenum de Statu, 1788—
Sequel to C. Curtis's Paper, 1792—Curtius rescued
from the Gulph, in Answer to Parr (by R. Cumberland),
scarce, 1792—Letter from Irenopolis to Eleutheropolis,
Birm. 1792, *half bound* *in 1 vol.*
895 Pashley (R.) Travels in Crete, 2 vol. LARGE PAPER, *india
proof plates* *Cambridge*, 1837
896 Pasquillorum Tomi duo (Versibus et soluta Oratione)
edente C. S. Curione, 2 parts in 1, *blue morocco extra,
gilt edges* *Eleutheropoli*, 1544
*** Very scarce. Heinsius gave 100 ducats for his copy,
which he considered unique.
897 Paston Letters (1422-1509), edited by J. Gairdner, 3 vol.
1872-75
898 Paul (St.) Life and Epistles, by W. J. Conybeare and
J. S. Howson, 2 vol. *plates, cloth, uncut* 1859
899 Pauli (R.) Bilder aus Alt England, *Gotha*, 1860—Tholuck
(A.) Stunden Christlicher Andacht, *Hamburg*, 1841—
Unverfälschter Liedersegen, *Berlin*, 1851—Homer's
Odyssee von W. Jordan, *Frankfurt*, 1875 ; and others,
German *a parcel*
900 Payn (J.) Literary Recollections, *portrait* 1884
901 Peacock (Dean G.) Life of Dr. T. Young, *portrait* 1855
902 Pearson (C. H.) History of England during the early and
middle Ages, 2 vol. 2 *autograph letters of the author
added, cloth, uncut* 1867

903 Pearson (Bp. J.) Minor Theological Works, with Life, by E. Churton, 2 vol. *portrait, 2 autograph letters of Churton added* *Oxford,* 1844
904 Pearson (Bp. J.) Exposition of the Creed *Camb.* 1859
905 Pegge (S.) Anonymiana, *half calf gilt,* 1818—Melcombe (G. Bubb Dodington, Lord) Diary, *Salisbury,* 1784— Matriculation Papers of London University, 1841-43— Müller (Max) on the Stratification of Language, 1868 —Lewis (W.) Chess for Beginners, *numerous diagrams,* 1835—Erasmus (D.) Pilgrimages to St. Mary of Walsingham and St. Thomas of Canterbury, *frontispiece,* 1849 ; and 5 others (10)
906 Pepys (S.) Diary and Correspondence, 5 vol. *portraits and plates, cloth* 1848
907 Percy (Bp. T.) Reliques of Ancient English Poetry, 3 vol. 1844
908 Percy (Bp. T.) Folio Manuscript of Ballads and Romances, with Loose and Humorous Songs, edited by J. W. Hales and F. J. Furnivall, 4 vol. in 7, *uncut* 1867
909 Perez de Hita (Gines) Guerras Civiles de Granada, 4 vol. *Granada,* 1847-50—Samaniego (F. M.) Fabulas en Verso, *Sevilla,* 1856—Nuevo Testamento trad. por C. de Valera, 1858—El Cid, Romances, *Palma,* 1844—Del Mar (E.) Spanish Grammar, 1853—Elwes (A.) Spanish Grammar, 1852—Witcomb (C. and H.) Spanish and English Conversations, *Paris,* 1857—Monteith (A. H.) Spanish without a Master, 1844 (11)
910 Perkins Library Sale Catalogue, LARGE PAPER, *plates, MS. prices and names, half calf gilt* 1873
911 Perry (W. C.) Greek and Roman Sculpture, 268 *woodcuts, ornamented cloth, uncut, top edge gilt* 1882
912 Petrarca (F.) Rime, *Geneva,* 1851—Tasso (T.) Gerusalemme Liberata, 4 vol. *portrait, half morocco, uncut, top edges gilt, Parigi,* 1835—Machiavelli (N.) Istorie Fiorentine, 3 vol. *frontispiece, half bound, ib.* 1825— Tasso (T.) Aminta, *half calf gilt, ib.* 1828—Guarini (B.) Pastor Fido, *portrait, ib.* 1835—Manzoni (A.) Opere Poetiche, *portrait, ib.* 1840 (11)
913 Petronii Arbitri Satyricon et Poetarum Carmina non dissimilis Argumenti, *old red morocco, gilt edges* *Lutetiæ,* 1587
914 Phalaridis Epistolæ Gr. et Lat. cum Notis C. Boyle, LARGE PAPER, *frontispiece, old gilt calf* *Oxonia,* 1695
915 Philemonis Lexicon Technologicum, Græce edidit C. Burney, *half calf gilt* 1812
916 Phillips (S.) Caleb Stukeley, *with illustrations of Dalziel, autograph letter of G. E. Paget added* 1854

F 2

917 Piazza (C. B.) Eorterologia, *Roma*, 1858—Diario Romano per 1878-80, *ib.* 1878-80—Mirabilia Romæ edidit G. Parthey, *Berolini*, 1869 (3)

918 Pico (G. F.) Life of Giovanni Pico della Mirandola, with three of his Letters translated by Sir T. More, edited with Notes by J. M. Rigg, *vellum* 1890

919 Piggott (J.) Truth without Fiction, or Two Oxford Students, *plates*, 1837—Radcliffe (Ann) Mysteries of Udolpho, *woodcuts*, 1824—Bramston (F. T.) Job Simmons and Domleight not Domlet, 2 vol. *frontispiece and view of Oxford, with author's autograph letter*, 1890— Auerbach (B.) Professor's Wife, 1851 — Rosette and Miriam, 1837 (6)

920 PINDARI CARMINA ; Calimachi Hymni ; Dionysius de Situ Orbis ; et Licophronis Alexandra ; Græce, FIRST EDITION, *old red morocco* *Venetiis, Aldus*, 1513
*** Rare. Sir J. Thorold's copy sold for £11.

921 Pitcairn (E. H.) Golden Thread 1887

922 Plato's Gorgias, literally translated by E. M. Cope, *translator's autograph inscription* *Cambridge*, 1864

923 Platonis Opera Omnia, Græce cum Notis I. Bekkeri et Variorum, 10 vol. *bust, calf extra* 1826

924 Plinii Naturalis Historia cum Indice, 4 vol. *old gilt calf* *Venetiis, Aldus*, 1540, *et Index* 1538

925 Plutarchi Vitæ et Opera Moralia, Græce, 6 vol. *calf, gilt edges, Excudebat H. Stephanus*, 1572—Vitæ parallelæ Latine cum Appendice Interprete H. Cruserio, 4 vol. *vellum, gilt edges, ib.* 1572—Opuscula H. Stephano et Diversis Interpretibus, 3 vol. *vellum, gilt edges, ib.* 1572
13 *vol.*

926 Plutarchus de sera Numinis Vindicta Gr. et Lat. *autograph and MS. notes of Gilbert Wakefield, vellum, Lugd. Bat.* 1772—Æsopicarum Fabularum Collectio Gr. et Lat. *Oxoniæ*, 1718—Musæus de Herone et Leandro Gr. et Lat. cura J. Schraderi, *calf, Leovardiæ*, 1742 (3)

927 Plutarch's Lives, translated by J. and W. Langhorne, 6 vol. *portrait, calf extra* 1819

928 Poems. Bosanquet (H.) Verses recited at Oxford, 15 June, 1814—Frere (J. H.) Whistlecraft, 1817—Praed (W. M.) Australasia, *Camb.* 1823—Bosanquet (H.) Song and Son of Urania, *privately printed and dedicated to Mrs. H. Luard*, 1837—Neale (J. M.) Ruth and Hymn on the Cattle Plague, *Camb.* 1860—Bickersteth (E. H.) Winged Words, *printed on various coloured papers*, 1861—Kingsley (C.) Installation Ode, *Camb.* 1862—Delapryme (C.) Ars Cœnandi, *with author's autograph inscription, privately printed*, 1868 ; and others in the Volume, *half calf gilt* *in* 1 *vol.*

929 POETÆ MINORES GRÆCI cum Scholiis Græce edente T.
Gaisford, 4 vol. in 3, LARGE PAPER, *russia extra, gilt
edges, by C. Lewis*　　　　　　　　　　*Oxon.* 1814
  ** Only 50 copies printed. Williams's copy sold for £11 10s.
930 Poetæ Latini Veteres, 2 vol. *half vellum, Florentiæ,* 1829
—Gnomici Poetæ Græci edente R. F. P. Brunck, *Argent.*
1784　　　　　　　　　　　　　　　　　　　　(3)
931 Poetarum veterum Latinorum, quorum Opera non extant,
Fragmenta (Ennii, Pacunii, Accii, Lucilii aliorumque),
calf extra　　　　　　　　　　*H. Stephanus,* 1564
932 Poets (British) Bell's Edition, 124 vol. in 61, *portraits
and plates, calf gilt*　　　　　　　　　　　1807
933 Pomponius Mela. Julius Solinus. Itinerarium Antonini
Aug. Vibius Sequester. P. Victor de Regionibus Urbis
Romæ et Dionysius Afer de Situ Orbis, Prisciano Interprete, *vellum*　　　　　　*Venetiis, Aldus,* 1518
  ** Very rare. Sir J. Thorold's copy sold for £10 5s.
934 Pope (A.) Poetical Works, with Life by Dr. S. Johnson,
2 vol. *portrait, half russia,* 1811—Select British Poets,
portraits, half bound, 1810—Schiller (F.) Don Carlos
and Robbers, 2 vol. 1798-99　　　　　　　(5)
935 Porson (R.) Tracts and Miscellaneous Cricticisms collected
by T. Kidd, 1815—Correspondence, edited by H. R.
Luard, *Cambridge,* 1867　　　　　　　　(2)
936 Prentiss (Mrs. E.) Stepping Heavenward, *n. d.*—Avrillon
(M.) Guide for passing Lent Holily, with Preface by E.
B. Pusey, 1844—Wake (Lady) Bible Reading on the
Life of Christ, vol. III and IV, in 1 vol. 1855—Pentateuch, with Commentary, *maps and plans,* 1876—
Apocrypha, with Commentary, 1880—Horst (J. M.)
Paradise of the Christian Soul, vol. II, 1847　　(6)

QUARTO.

937 Mabillon (J.) Museum Italicum, 2 vol. *old calf*
Lut. Paris. 1724
938 Maittaire (M.) Annales Typographici ab Artis inventæ
Origine ad Annum 1664, 4 vol. *Amst. Hagæ et Lond.*
1733-41, *with First Edition Hagæ,* 1719 *added*　5 *vol.*
939 Manucci (Aldo) Lettere Volgari, *brown morocco extra,
borders of gold, gilt edges*　　　　*Roma, Aldo,* 1592
940 Martyrologium Romanum, *calf gilt*　　　*Romæ,* 1845
941 Mathias (T.) Pursuits of Literature, LARGE PAPER,
author's autograph letter added, half calf extra　1812
942 Mathematical Tracts by Talbot, Moseley, Davies, Whewell,
Russell, O'Brien and Ellis, Rothman, Mallet, Baily,
Munro, Scott and Shilleto, 18 Tracts in 1 vol. *plates,
mostly presentation copies, with author's autograph inscriptions, half calf gilt*　　　　　　　1836-57

943 Merigot (J.) Views and Ruins in Rome and its Vicinity, *open-letter proofs, russia extra, borders of gold*   1797

944 Middleton (C.) Bibliothecæ Cantabrigiensis ordinandæ Methodus, *Cantab.* 1723—Lewis (J.) Account of Suffragan Bishops in England, 1785—Hartshorne (C. H.) Itinerary of Edward II, *printed for private distribution,* 1861 — Lechler (G. V.) Roberte Grosseteste Bischof von Lincoln, *Leipzig,* 1867—Ingleby (C. M.) Was Thomas Lodge an Actor? *facsimile of P. Henslowe's letter,* 1868—Fullerton (Lady Georgiana) In Memoriam Baron C. von Hügel, *with Baroness de Hügel's autograph inscription,* 1884—Jessopp (A.) Fragments of Primitive Liturgies, *printed for private circulation,* 1872—Field (F.) Otium Norwicense Pars altera, *Oxonii,* 1876 — Jebb (R. C.) Ode Græca Universitate Bononiensi, 1888 ; and other Tracts in the Volume, *half calf gilt*

945 Mill (G. H.) Prælectio Theologica in Scholis Cantabrigiensibus, *author's inscription, russia extra, uncut*
Cantab. 1843

946 Mill (G. H.) Prælectio Theologica in Scholis Cantabrigiensibus   *ib.* 1843

947 Milton (J.) Allegro and Penseroso, 30 *illustrations*
Art Union, 1848

948 Missale de Arbuthnott secundum usum Ecclesiæ S. Andreæ in Scotia, with Preface by Bp. A. P. Forbes
Burntisland, 1864

949 Montucla (J. F.) Histoire des Mathematiques, 4 vol. *portraits of Montucla and La Lande and plates, russia extra, with Trinity College arms in gold on sides*
Paris, 1799-1802

950 Morell (T.) Lexicon Græco-Prosodiacum auctum ab E. Maltby, 2 *portraits, russia*   *Cantab.* 1815

951 Munro (H. A. J.) Translations into Latin and Greek Verse, *vellum*   *Cambridge,* 1884

952 Neperi (J.) Mirifici Logarithmorum Canonis Descriptio, *the rarest Edition, pp. 14 and 15 erroneously numbered 22 and 23, and before the Admonitio was printed on reverse of last leaf, woodcuts, Porson's copy with the Admonitio in his handwriting, and with an autograph letter of W. R. Macdonald pointing out how to distinguish the two editions of* 1614, EXTREMELY RARE, *Edinb.* 1614

953 Nasmith (J.) Catalogus Manuscriptorum, quos Collegio Corporis Christi legavit M. Parker, Archiepiscopus Cantuariensis, *uncut*   *Cantab.* 1777

954 Newcome (H.) Diary (1661-63) edited by T. Heywood, *printed for Chetham Society,* 1849 — Autobiography, edited by R. Parkinson, 2 vol. *ib.* 1852   (3)

955 Newcome (P.) History of the Abbey of St. Alban, FINE
PAPER, *map and plates, old gilt calf* 1795
956 NEWTONI (IS.) OPERA OMNIA LATINA et Anglica Commentariis illustrabat S. Horsley, 5 vol. *plates, with facsimile of Newton's Letter to Professor Cotes added, russia
extra, with Trinity College arms in gold on sides*, 1779-85
957 Nicandri Theriaca et Alexipharmaca, cum Scholiis, Græce,
2 vol. in 1, *fine copy in red morocco extra, gilt edges*
Venetiis, Aldus, 1522-23
** Scarce. Sir J. Thorold's copy sold for £4 15s.
958 Nonni Dionysiaca, Græce, cura G. Falkenburgii, *autograph
of G. Burges, vellum Antverpiæ, C. Plantinus*, 1569
959 North (Hon. Roger) Autobiography, edited by A. Jessopp,
portrait, with autograph letter of editor added
Norwich, 1887
960 Notes and Queries, from January to June, 1852, and 9
Nos. for 1858 *a parcel*
961 Origenis Hexapla, Græce adhibita Versione Syro-Hexaplari
edente F. Field, 2 vol. in 5 *Oxonii*, 1867-75
962 Parisiensis Universitatis Chartularium edentibus H. Denifle
et A. Chatelain Tomus I (1200-1286), *uncut, with autograph letter of Denifle added Paris*, 1889
963 Pegge (S.) Life of Robert Grosseteste, the celebrated
Bishop of Lincoln, and Memoirs of Roger de Wescham,
Dean of Lincoln, Bishop of Coventry and Lichfield,
2 vol. in 1, *calf extra, gilt edges, by F. Bedford*
1793 *and* 1761
964 Photii Lexicon Græcum e Codice Galeano descripit R.
Porsonus, 2 vol. LARGE PAPER, *with a fragment of Porson's autograph burnt MS. added, half morocco, g. e.* 1822
965 Platina (B.) Vite de' Pontefici e da Sisto IV sino el Benedetto XIII scritte da O. Panvinio ed altri, 2 vol. *woodcut portraits, vellum Venezia*, 1730
966 Plauti Fragmenta inedita. Item ad Terentium Commen-
tationes et Picturæ ineditæ Inventore A. Maio, LARGE
PAPER, *russia extra, gilt gaufré edges Mediolani*, 1815
967 Poetry of the Anti-Jacobin, *autograph of Archdeacon F.
Wrangham, half calf extra* 1801
968 Pontificum Romanorum Regesta ab condita Ecclesia ad
Annum 1198 edidit P. Jaffé, *Berolini*, 1851—Regista ab
Anno 1198 ad Annum 1304 edidit A. Potthast, 2 vol.
ib. 1874-75, *half calf gilt* 3 *vol.*
969 Porphyrii Homericæ Quæstiones et de Nympharum Antro
in Odyssea Opusculum, Græce, FIRST EDITION, *fine copy
in old veau marbré, gilt edges Romæ*, 1518
** Extremely rare. Sir M. Sykes's copy sold for £9 9s.
970 Pronti (D.) Vedute di Roma, 2 vol. in 1, 170 *views, half
red morocco Roma, s. a.*

971 Pulci (Luigi) Morgante Maggiore in ottava Rima, *portrait, vellum, uncut* *Firenze*, 1732
972 Punch from July 1841 to December 1852 with Almanacks, 12 vol. in 6, *numerous humorous illustrations, half morocco, gilt edges* 1841-52
973 Pusey (E. B.) Minor Prophets with a Commentary, *half morocco* *Oxford*, 1860
974 Raine (J.) St. Cuthbert, with Account of the State of his Remains upon the Opening of his Tomb, *plates, half morocco, uncut* *Durham*, 1828
975 Roccha (A. *Episcopus Tagastensis*) de Campanis, *very scarce (see MS. Note), vellum* *Romæ*, 1612
976 Roscoe (W.) Life of Lorenzo de' Medici, 2 vol. *portrait, old calf, backs broken* 1796
977 Rosetta Stone by M. Raper, H. Turner, C. G. Hayne and Taylor Combe, *plates*, 1804—Monk (J. H.) Concio ad Clerum, *Cantab.* 1827—Stukeley (W.) Account of Croyland Abbey, *plates, Ashby-de-la-Zouch*, 1856—Munro (H. A.) on Inscription at Cirta, *Camb.* 1861—Cooper (C. H.) Account of Trinity College, *views*—Marsden (J. H.) Memoirs of W. Martin Leake, *Printed for private circulation only*, 1864—Pauli (R.) über Bischof Grosseteste und Adam von Marsh, *Tübingen*, 1864—Willis (R.) Worcester Cathedral Crypt and Chapter House, *plates*, 1863—Cooper (C. H.) on Percy Herbert Lord Powis, *n. d.*—Field (F.) Otium Norwicense, *Oxonii*, 1864, *half calf gilt* *in* 1 *vol.*
978 Rossi (G. G. de) Scherzi Poetici e Pittorici, LARGE PAPER, *coloured plates, half morocco, uncut, Parma, Bodoni*, 1795
979 Rossi (G. B.) Piante icnografiche e prospettive di Roma anteriori al Secole XVI, *Roma*, 1879, *with various Engravings in a roll*

ROXBURGHE CLUB PUBLICATIONS.

980 Vox Populi, Vox Dei, a Complaynt of the Comons against Taxes (in Verse), **black letter**, *presentation copy to R. Addams, with Dr. T. F. Dibdin's autograph inscription, half Roxburghe, uncut* 1821
*** Presented to the Members by Sir J. Littledale, who when raised to the Bench destroyed every copy he could secure.
981 Owl and Nightingale, Poem of the XIIth Century, edited by J. Stevenson, *half red morocco* 1838
*** Presented to the Members by Sir S. R. Glynne, Bart.
982 Roxburghe Revels and other relative Papers including Answers to the Attack on the Memory of J. Haslewood with Specimens of his Literary Productions, *uncut* *Edinb.* 1837
*** Printed for private circulation.

Roxburghe Club Publications—*continued.*

983 Black Prince, an historical Poem in French by the Chandos Herald, with Translation and Notes by Rev. H. O. Coxe, *autograph letter of Coxe added, half Roxburghe, uncut,* 1842
₊ Printed by the Roxburghe Club.

984 Wey (W.) Itineraries to Jerusalem in 1458 and 1462 and St. James of Compostella in 1456, edited by G. Williams, with coloured Map of the Holy Land illustrating the Itinerarie, 2 vol. *half Roxburghe, uncut*   1857-67
₊ Printed by the Clnb.

985 Edward VI, Literary Remains with Notes and Memoir by J. G. Nichols, 2 vol. *half Roxburghe, uncut*   1867
₊ Printed by the Club.

986 Guillaume de Deguileville, Pilgrimage of the Lyf of the Manhode, edited by W. A. Wright, *half Roxburghe, uncut*   1869
₊ Printed by the Club.

987 Liber Regalis seu Ordo consecrandi Regem solum, Reginam cum Rege et Reginam solam. Item Rubrica de Regis Exequiis, *facsimile, half Roxburghe, uncut*   1870
₊ Presented to the Members by Earl Beauchamp.

988 Hooke (Col. N.) Correspondence (1703-7), edited by Rev. W. D. Macray, 2 vol. *half Roxburghe, uncut*   1870-71
₊ Printed by the Club.

989 Mystère de Saint Louis Roi de France publié par F. Michel, *facsimile, half Roxburghe, uncut*   1871
₊ Printed by the Club.

990 Partonope of Blois, Fragment from Lord Delamere's Manuscript, *facsimile, half Roxburghe, uncut*   1873
₊ Printed by the Club.

991 Hystorie of the moste noble Knight Plasidas, and other rare Pieces, collected into one Book by S. Pepys, *illuminated facsimiles, half Roxburghe, uncut*   1873
₊ Printed by the Club.

992 Apocalypse represented by Figures reproduced in Facsimile, *coloured plates, half Roxburghe, uncut*   1876
₊ Printed for the Club, with Preface by H. O. Coxe.

993 Barnfield (R.) Complete Poems, edited, with Introduction and Notes, by Rev. A. B. Grosart, *view of Norbury House, half Roxburghe, uncut*   1876
₊ Printed by the Club.

994 Poems from Sir K. Digby's Paper in Possession of H. A. Bright, *portrait of Digby and facsimile, half Roxburghe, uncut*   1877
₊ Presented to Members by H. A. Bright.

ROXBURGHE CLUB PUBLICATIONS—*continued.*

995 Harington (Sir John) Tract on the Succession to the
    Crown (1602), *portrait, half Roxburghe, uncut*   1880
    ** Printed by the Club.

996 Lamport Garland, from the Library of Sir C. E. Isham,
    Bart. edited by C. Edmonds, *coats of arms, half Rox-*
    burghe, uncut   1881
    ** Printed by the Club.

997 Hall (J.) Kings Prophecie, edited by Rev. W. E. Buckley,
    view of Halstead Rectory, half Roxburghe, uncut   1882
    ** Printed by the Club.

998 Edwards (T.) Cephalus and Procris, Narcissus, edited by
    Rev. W. E. Buckley, *half Roxburghe, uncut*   1882
    ** Printed by the Club.

999 Quatuor Sermones reprinted from Caxton's first Edition,
    facsimile, half Roxburghe, uncut   1883
    ** Printed by the Club.

1000 Beaumont Papers, edited by Rev. W. D. Macray, *fac-*
    simile, half Roxburghe, uncut   1884

1001 Ruskin (J.) Notes on his Collection of Drawings by J.
    M. W. Turner, LARGE PAPER, *illustrated by 35 plates and*
    map, half morocco, uncut, top edge gilt   1878
1002 Rastell (J.) Pastime of People, or Chronicles of divers
    Realms, especially England, edited by T. F. Dibdin, *fac-*
    simile woodcuts of the portraits of Popes, Emperors, &c.
    and Kings of England, old calf, rebacked   1811
1003 Rusticæ Rei Scriptores (Cato, Terentius Varro, Colu-
    mella, Palladius, &c.) PRINTED ON AZURE PAPER, *gilt*
    vellum, with autograph letter from J. K. Ingram added,
    extremely rare if not unique   *Venetiis, Aldus,* 1533

FOLIO.

1004 Menologium Græcorum, Gr. et Lat. Cura A. Cardinalis
    Albani, 3 vol. *numerous illustrations, vellum*
    Urbini, 1727
1005 Monumenta Germaniæ Historica, Scriptorum Tomus
    XXVIII, *calf gilt*   *Hannoveræ,* 1888
    ** This volume contains the Extracts "Ex Rerum Angli-
    carum Scriptoribus Sæculi XIII edente F. Liebermann.

1006 Monumenta Historica Brittanica, with Notes by H. A.
    Petrie assisted by Rev. J. Sharpe, edited by Sir T. D.
    Hardy, *autograph letter of Hardy added, russia extra*
    1848

1007 Nider (J.) Exposicio Decalogi, *stained, red morocco, gilt edges, by Derome*
    s. l. & a. sed Coloniæ, Ulricus Zell, circa 1470

1008 ORVIETO. Stampe del Duomo, 38 *fine engravings, with 3 photographs added, half russia*   *Roma,* 1791

1009 Oxford University Commission Report, *half calf gilt*
                    1852

1010 Palæographical Society's Facsimiles of Ancient Manuscripts, edited by E. A. Bond and E. M. Thompson, 13 Parts, 260 *facsimiles, uncut*   1873-83

1011 Parker Cantuariensis Archiepiscopi (M.) de Antiquitate Britannicæ Ecclesiæ et Privilegiis Ecclesiæ Cantuariensis cum Archiepiscopis ejusdem LXX Historia recensente S. Drake, adjectis Augustini Vita et Academiæ Historia Cantabrigiensis, LARGE PAPER, *portrait of Parker by Vertue and plates, old gilt russia*   1729

1012 PAUSANIAS, Græce, Cura M. Musuri, FIRST EDITION, *fine copy in old calf, gilt edges*   *Venetiis, Aldus,* 1516
 ** Rare. Sir J. Thorold's copy sold for £14 5s.

1013 Pearson (C. H.) Historical Maps of England during the first thirteen Centuries, *coloured maps, half morocco, uncut, top edge gilt*   1869

1014 Perrault (C.) Contes des Fées, *india proof illustrations by G. Doré*   *Paris,* 1862

1015 Philonis Judæi Opera, Græce   *Paris. A. Turnebus,* 1552

1016 Philostratorum Opera omnia. Accessere Apollonii Tyanensis Epistolæ ; Eusebii Liber adversus Hieroclem; et Callistrati Descriptio Statuarum. Omnia Gr. et Lat. cum Notis G. Olearii, *old stamped calf*   *Lipsiæ,* 1709

1017 Photii Bibliotheca, Græce cum Notis D. Hœschelii, FIRST EDITION, *fine copy in brown morocco extra, gilt edges*
            Aug. Vind. 1601

1018 PINDARI CARMINA, Gr. et Lat. curantibus R. West et R. Welsted, LARGE PAPER, *portrait, with a specimen of the Caligraphy of J. Thomasen added, very fine copy, ruled, old calf, with arms of Lord Clare in gold on sides*
             Oxonii, 1697

1019 Platonis Opera M. Ficino Interprete. Accedit ejusdem M. Ficini Platonica Theologia de Immortalitate Animorum, *slightly wormed, old gilt russia, by Roger Payne, with Wodhull arms in gold on sides*   *Venetiis,* 1491
 ** Printed at the expense of A. Toresanus de Asula, the father-in-law of Aldus. Sir J. Thorold's copy sold for £3.

1020 PLATONIS OPERA OMNIA, Græce, FIRST EDITION, *very fine copy in blue morocco, borders of gold, gilt edges, by C. Smith, with Aldine anchor stamped in gold on sides*
Venetiis, Aldus, 1513

₊ One of the most important of the Aldine Publications but extremely rare, in fine condition. Sir J. Thorold's copy sold for £32.

1021 Plutarchi Vitæ paralellæ, Græce, FIRST EDITION, *with the life of Sylla often deficient, orange morocco extra*
Florentiæ, P. Junta, 1517

₊ Scarce. The Wodhull copy sold for £3 15s.

1022 Plutarchi Opuscula Moralia, Græce, FIRST EDITION, *autograph and MS. notes of G. Burges, russia, gilt edges, by Roger Payne, rebacked* *Venetiis, Aldus,* 1509

₊ Very rare. Sir M. Sykes's copy sold for £8 18s. 6d.

1023 Poliphili Hypnerotomachia, Facsimiles of the 168 Woodcuts in the Aldine Edition of 1499, with Notices and Descriptions by J. W. Apell, *photo-lithographs* 1888

1024 Politiani (Angeli) Miscellaneorum Centuriæ, *vellum*
Florentiæ, 1489

1025 Pybus (C. S.) The Sovereign addressed to Paul Emperour of Russia, LARGE PAPER, *fine portrait, plate of the crown in three states, with curious Pybussiana (including cancelled leaves) in Manuscript added at end, half calf, gilt edges* 1800

1026 Raffaele Sanzio I Freschi delle Loggie Vaticane, *engraved in outline by A. Becchio and G. Camilli, half vellum, uncut* *Roma,* 1840

1027 Redfarn (W. B.) Original Sketches of Old Cambridge, 9 Parts, 26 *plates* *Cambridge,* 1875-76

1028 Reid (G. W.) Works of the Italian Engravers of the XVth Century (Monte Sancto di Dio, Dante and Petrarch), reproduced in Facsimile by Photo-Intaglio, with Introduction, *plates, half bound, uncut* 1884

1029 Report on Revenues and Management of certain Colleges and Schools, 4 vol. 1864

1030 Report I and II of Commissioners on Public Worship 1867-68

1031 Reports on Historical Manuscripts, 4 vol. in 5 1870-74

1032 Report I & II on University Tests, 1871—Special Report on Oxford and Cambridge University Education Bill (3)

1033 Rhetores Græci, *very rare* *Venetiis, Aldus,* 1508

FOURTH DAY'S SALE.

OCTAVO ET INFRA.

LOT
1034 Prescott (W. H.) Works, viz. History of Ferdinand and
Isabella the Catholic of Spain, 3 vol. *portrait,* 1849—
History of the Conquest of Mexico, with Life of H.
Cortes, 3 vol. 1850—History of the Conquest of Peru,
3 vol. 1850—History of Philip II, 3 vol. *portraits,* 1879,
cloth, uncut   12 *vol.*

1035 Proisy d'Eppe (Comte de) Dictionnaire des Girouettes,
coloured frontispiece, calf   *Paris,* 1815

1036 Prothero (G. W.) Simon de Montfort, Earl of Leicester,
author's autograph inscription   1877

1037 Prudentius. Preface and Hymns for Cock Crow, Day-
Break and Before Sleep, *Cambridge,* 1887—Hymns for
Cock-Crow and Day-Break, in Latin and English, by G.
Morison, 1887, in 1 vol. *half calf gilt*—Hymns for
Christmas Day and Epiphany, and Hymn for Burial of
the Dead, by G. Morison, 2 vol. *ib.* 1888-89   (3)

1038 Pryme (G.) Autobiographic Sketches, *pen and ink portrait added*   *Cambridge,* 1870

1039 Psalmanazar (G.) Memoirs, *mezzotint portrait,* 1764—
Description of Formosa, *plates,* 1704   (2)

1040 Pusey (E. B.) Letter to the Archbp. of Canterbury, *Oxford,* 1842 ; and 7 Single Sermons, by Pusey   (8)

1041 Pusey (E. B.) Letter on Tendency to Romanism, *Oxford,*
1840—Is healthful Reunion impossible? *ib.* 1870—
Letter to Newman on Love to Theotekos and the Imma-
culate Conception, 1869—Sermons, *Oxford,* 1848—
Eleven Addresses during a Retreat of the Companions
of the Love of Jesus, *Plymouth,* 1868   (5)

1042 Pusey (E. B.) Parochial Sermons, vol. II, *Oxford,* 1853
—University Sermons, *with author's autograph letter,*
ib. 1872—Occasional Parochial Sermons, *ib.* 1865   (3)

1043 Pusey (E. B.) Truth and Office of the English Church,
1865—Letter to Bp. of London in Explanation of W.
Dodsworth's Statements, 1851—Renewed Explanation,
1851—What is Faith as to everlasting Punishment?
Oxford, 1880—Church of England leaves her Children
free to whom to open their Griefs, 1850   (5)

1044 Quatremère de Quincy (M.) Histoire de Raphael, *portrait and facsimile, half gilt vellum*   *Paris,* 1824

1045 Quarterly Review, from February 1809 to January 1824 inclusive, 30 vol. *Mr. Beckford's copy with his autograph notes on 34 pages, uncut, top edges gilt,* 1810-24 *and vol.* 31, 32, 33, 38, 39, 41, 46, 58, 124 and 125, 10 vol. *half calf,* 1825-68 **40 vol.**

1046 Quinti Calabri Derelictorum ab Homero Libri XIV. Tryphiodorus de Trojæ Excidio et Coluthus de Raptu Helenæ. Omnia Græce, *fine copy in stamped pigskin* *Venetiis, Aldus, s. a. circa* 1505

  ** Very rare. Sir J. Thorold's copy sold for £9.

1047 Quiz (The), by a Society of Gentlemen (Sir R. K. Porter, T. F. Dibdin, W. H. Winter and others), 51 Nos. in 1 vol. *all published, frontispiece by Sir R. K. Porter, whose portrait is added, with names of contributors in pencil* **n. d.**

  ** Dr. Dibdin mentions the work as most rare, nearly the entire stock having been destroyed by fire, which caused the publication to cease.

1048 Randolph (T.) Poetical and Dramatic Works, with Notes by W. C. Hazlitt, *portrait and view* 1873

1049 Ranke (L.) History of the Popes of Rome during XVIth and XVIIth Centuries, translated by Sarah Austin, 3 vol. *calf extra* 1840

1050 Redding (Cyrus) Memoirs of remarkable Misers, 2 vol. 1863—Merryweather (F. S.) Lives and Anecdotes of Misers, 1850 (3)

1051 Reiskens (J. J.) Selbst aufgesetzte Lebensbeschreibung, *Porson's copy, with long autograph letter in Latin from Reiske to Brunck added* *Leipzig,* 1783

1052 Renouard (A. A.) Catalogue de la Bibliotheque d'un Amateur, 4 vol. LARGE PAPER, *half russia, uncut, top edges gilt* *Paris,* 1819

  ** This copy sold for £2 10s. in Mr. Beckford's sale.

1053 Renouard (A. A.) Annales de l'Imprimerie des Alde, 3 vol. LARGE PAPER, *portraits and facsimiles, half morocco, uncut, top edges gilt* *Paris,* 1825

1054 Renouard (A. A.) Catalogue de sa Bibliothèque, *with printed prices, half morocco, uncut, top edge gilt* *ib.* 1854-55

1055 Riley (H. T.) Memorials of London and London Life (1276-1419), *uncut* 1868

1056 Ritson (J.) Pieces of Ancient Popular Poetry, *illustrations by Stothard, old gilt calf* 1791

1057 Robert de Torigni, Abbé de Mont-Saint Michel, Chronique suivie de divers Opuscules historiques de cet Auteur et de plusieurs Religieux de la même Abbaye. Le tous publié par L. Delisle, 2 vol. *autograph letter of editor added, calf gilt* *Rouen,* 1872-73

1058 Robertson (J. C.) Becket Archbishop of Canterbury, *frontispiece, with autograph letter of the author added, half red morocco* 1859

1059 Robertson (J. C.) History of the Christian Church, 8 vol. *cloth, uncut* 1874-75

1060 Robertson (W.) Works, with Life, by Rev. A. Stewart, 12 vol. *portrait and maps, russia extra* 1820

1061 Robinson (H. C.) Diary, Reminiscences and Correspondence, selected and edited by T. Sadler, 3 vol. *portrait, half morocco extra* 1869

1062 Rogers (Capt. Woodes) Life aboard a British Privateer in the Time of Queen Anne, *illustrations by R. C. Leslie* 1889

1063 Rogers (S.) Human Life, FIRST EDITION, *calf extra, scarce*, 1819—Cowper (W.) Poems, 2 vol. *portrait added, half calf gilt*, 1803—Collins (W.) Poetical Works, *portrait, W. Pickering*, 1830—Vaughan (H.) Sacred Poems, *W. Pickering*, 1847—Devil's Walk, by R. Porson, *illustrations by R. Cruikshank*, 1830 (6)

1064 Roland (Madame) Mémoires, 2 vol. *portrait, Paris*, 1823 —Montreux par Rambert, Lebert, Dufour, Forel et Chavanney, *map and illustrations by G. Doré, Bachelin, &c. Neuchatel*, 1877—Stael (Mad. de) Dix Années d'Exil, *half calf extra, Paris*, 1845—Lamartine (A. de) Raphael, *Bruxelles*, 1849—La Bruyère (J. de) Caractères, *portrait, Paris*, 1869—Stael (Mad. de) Corinne, *portrait, ib.* 1847 ; and 3 others, French (10)

1065 Roscii (J.) Triumphus Martyrum in Templo D. Stephani Cœlii Montis expressus, *plates by J. B. de Cavalleriis, presentation copy*, " Episcopo Venusino," *with author's autograph inscription, morocco, gilt edges, by C. Smith Romæ*, 1587

*** This copy sold for £2 in Mr. Beckford's sale.

1066 Rose (H. J.) Inscriptiones Græcæ vetustissimæ, *plates Cantab.* 1825

1067 Rosse (J. W.) Index of Dates, 2 vol. 1858-59

1068 Rossi (G. G. de) Vita di Angelica Kauffmann Pittrice, *portrait, half bound Firenze*, 1810

1069 Routh (M. J.) Reliquæ Sacræ, 5 vol. *uncut Oxonii*, 1846-48

1070 Royal and Historical Letters during the Reign of Henry IV, edited by Rev. F. C. Hingeston, vol. II (1405-13), *the cancelled volume, of which only 8 copies were preserved*, 1864—and Proof Sheets of Matthew Paris, with Dr. Luard's autograph corrections *a parcel*

1071 Royston (Viscount) Remains, with Life by Rev. H. Pepys (including Translation of Lycophron), *presentation copy*, " *with Lord Stuart de Rothesay's compliments* " 1838

1072 Ruffini (J.) Lorenzo Benoni, *Edinb.* 1853 — Doctor Antonio and a Quiet Nook in the Jura, 2 vol. *half calf extra, Leipzig,* 1861-67 (3)

1073 Ruskin (J.) The Two Paths, FIRST EDITION, *plates,* 1859

1074 Ruskin (J.) Elements of Perspective, FIRST EDITION, 1859

1075 Ruskin (J.) Bibliotheca Pastorum, vol. I, II and IV in 3 parts, *uncut* *Orpington,* 1876-85

1076 Ruskin (J.) Lectures on Art, *cloth, uncut, Oxford,* 1880

1077 Ruskin (J.) Poems, collected and edited by J. O. Wright, LARGE PAPER, *proof etching* *New York,* 1882

1078 Ruskin (J.) Præterita, Outlines of Scenes and Thoughts in my past Life, 2 vol. *steel engravings, half blue morocco extra, uncut, top edges gilt* *Orpington,* 1886-87

1079 Ruskin (J.) Notes on Royal Academy Pictures, 1875— Ethics of the Dust, *Orpington,* 1886—Stones of Venice, 2 vol. *ib.* 1884-85—Modern Painters, 2 vol. *ib.* 1883 (6)

1080 Russell (A. T.) Life of Bp. L. Andrewes, *Cambridge,* 1860

1081 Rymer's Fœdera. Syllabus, in English, of the Documents relating to England and other Kingdoms contained in the Collection, with Appendix and Index by Sir T. D. Hardy, 3 vol. 1869-85—Appendices A to E to C. P. Cooper's Report on Rymer's Fœdera, 3 vol. *facsimiles (several illuminated in colours),* 1869 (6)

1082 Sabrinæ Corolla in Hortulis Regiæ Scholæ Salopiensis, *Cantab.* 1859—Arundines Cami, edidit H. Drury, *ib.* 1846—Linwood (G.) Anthologia Oxoniensis, 1846 (3)

1083 Saillii (T.) Thesaurus Precum et Exercitiorum spiritualium, *plates, red morocco, gold tooling, silk linings, gilt edges* *Antverpiæ,* 1609

1084 Sallustii Belli Catilinarii et Jugurthini Historiæ, *blue morocco, uncut, top edge gilt, scarce* *Edinburgi, Laminis fusis,* 1744

1085 Sand (George, *i. e.* Madame Dudevant) La Daniella, 2 vol. in 1, *half vellum, Paris,* 1869—Lélia, 2 vol. in 1, *ib.* 1869 ; and 7 others by Madame Dudevant (9)

1086 Sandford (Bp. D.) Remains, 2 vol. *Edinb.* 1830

1087 Sarum Missal, in English (by A. H. Pearson) 1868

1088 Savage (J.) The Librarian, 3 vol. *half russia,* 1808-9— Memorabilia, *half calf gilt, Taunton,* 1820 (4)

1089 Saxon Chronicles (Two of the) ‛parallel with supplementary Extracts from the others, edited, with Notes and Glossary, by J. Earle, *facsimiles, cloth, uncut* *Oxford,* 1865

1090 Senecæ Tragœdiæ, *calf* *Venetiis, Aldus,* 1517

 ₊ Sir J. Thorold's copy sold for £2.

1091 Schimmelpenninck (M. A.) Select Memoirs of Port Royal, 3 vol. *half calf gilt* 1829

1092 Schlegel (A. W.) Lectures on Dramatic Art and Literature, *portrait, calf extra,* 1846—Whately (Archbp. R.)
Elements of Logic, 1855 — Whitaker's Almanack for
1881 and 1888—Gesta Romanorum, translated by C.
Swan, 1877   (5)

1093 Scotland Historians (Fordun, Wyntoun, Liber Plus-
cardensis, Innes, Adamnan, Life of St. Columba and
Lives of St. Ninian and S. Kentigern), 10 vol. *cloth,
uncut*   *Edinb.* 1871-74

1094 Scott (Sir Walter) Novels, viz. Waverley, 3 vol. *Edinb.*
1814—Guy Mannering, *second edition,* 3 vol. *ib.* 1815—
Antiquary, 3 vol. *ib.* 1816—Tales of my Landlord,
Four Series, 16 vol. *all* FIRST EDITIONS *except First
Series which is the second, ib.* 1817-18-19-32—Rob Roy,
3 vol. *ib.* 1818—Monastery and Abbot, 6 vol. *ib.* 1820
—Kenilworth, 3 vol. *ib.* 1821—Ivanhoe, 3 vol. *second
edition, ib.* 1820—Peveril of the Peak, 4 vol. *ib.* 1822—
Fortunes of Nigel, 3 vol. *ib.* 1822—The Pirate, 3 vol.
ib. 1822 — Quentin Durward, 3 vol. *ib.* 1823 — Red
Gauntlet, 3 vol. *ib.* 1824—St. Ronan's Well, 3 vol. *ib.*
1824—Tales of the Crusaders, 4 vol. *ib.* 1825—Wood-
stock, 3 vol. *ib.* 1826—Chronicles of the Canongate,
2 vol. *ib.* 1827—Anne of Geierstein, 3 vol. *ib.* 1829.
ALL FIRST EDITIONS *except Guy Mannering, First Series
of Tales of my Landlord and Ivanhoe*   71 *vol.*

1095 Scott (Sir W.) Poetical Works, 12 vol. *plates by Turner,
&c. uncut*   *Edinb.* 1833-34

1096 Scott (Sir W.) Biographies, 2 vol. *portraits, Edinb.* 1834;
and 9 others by Scott   (11)

1097 Scriptores Latini Rei metricæ MSS. Codicum Ope
subinde refinxit T. Gaisford, *Oxonii,* 1837—Buttmann
(P.) Intermediate Greek Grammar, *half calf gilt,* 1833
—Dawesii (R.) Miscellanea Critica cum Notis T. Kidd,
1827   (3)

1098 Scrivener (F. H.) Exact Transcript of the Codex
Augiensis, a Græco-Latin Manuscript of St. Paul's
Epistles in Trinity College Library, *facsimiles, with two
autograph letters of Scrivener added*   *Cambridge,* 1859

1099 Scrivener (F. H. A.) Plain Introduction to the Criticism
of the New Testament, *facsimiles, with autograph letter
of author added*   *ib.* 1883

1100 Sedgwick (A.) Life and Letters, by J. W. Clark and
T. M. Hughes, 2 vol. *portraits and plates, cloth, uncut*
ib. 1890

1101 Seeley (J. R.) Expansion of England, *presentation copy,
with author's autograph inscription*   1883
G

1102 Seeley (J. R.) Short History of Napoleon I, *portrait,*
1886—Lockhart (J. G.) History of Napoleon Buona-
parte, 2 vol. *plates,* 1829—Court and Camp of Buona-
parte, *portrait of Tallyrand,* 1829—Segur (Count P. de)
History of Napoleon's Expedition to Russia, 2 vol.
portraits and map, 1836—Bourrienne (F. de) Memoirs
of Napoleon, 4 vol. *plates, Edinb.* 1831   10 *vol.*
1103 Sermons. A Collection of 137 Sermons (*many rare*), by
various Clergymen (Bp. J. H. Monk, Bp. J. A. Selwyn,
C. H. Craufurd, W. J. Butler, Archdeacon Hodson, &c.)
in 5 vol. *half blue morocco*   1817-89
1104 Sermons and Charges. Gell (Bp. F.) Madras Charge,
Madras, 1863 ; and other Charges and Sermons by
France, Browne, Cooper, Bp. Perry, Davies, Smith,
Essington, Spry, Bather, Molyneux, Jenkins, &c.) *half
calf gilt*   *in* 1 *vol.*
1105 Sewell (Elizabeth M.) Tales by the Author of Amy
Herbert, vol. II to X, *wanting vol. I, or Amy Herbert*
1858-62
1106 Shakspeare (W.) Dramatic Works, with Glossary, *calf
extra, Chiswick,* 1823—Works, edited by W. G. Clark
and W. A. Wright, *Cambridge,* 1864; and 2 others (4)
1107 Shakespeare (W.) Works, edited by W. A. Wright, vol. I,
1891—First Act of Richard II, Private and Confidential
Specimen of a new Edition by W. G. Clark and H. R.
Luard, *extremely rare, Camb.* 1860—Ingleby (C. M.)
Shakspeare Fabrications, 1859—Farmer (R.) on the
Learning of Shakspeare, *portraits, half calf gilt,* 1821 (4)
1108 Shakspeariana. Six old Plays on which Shakspeare
founded his Measure for Measure, Comedy of Errors,
Taming the Shrew, King John, Henry IV and V and
Lear, 2 vol. *calf*   1779
1109 Shakspeariana. Hamilton (N. E. S. A.) Inquiry into
the Genuineness of the Manuscript Corrections in J. P.
Collier's Annotated Shakspere Folio, 1632, *facsimiles,*
1860—Collier (J. P.) Reply to Hamilton, 1860—Bray
(E.) Collier, Coleridge and Shakespeare, 1860—Hardy
(T. D.) Review of Shakespearian Controversy, 1860,
half calf gilt   *in* 1 *vol.*
1110 Sheepshanks (R.) Letter to Board of Visitors of Green-
wich Observatory in Reply to Babbage, *portrait,* 1860 ;
and other privately printed Tracts by R. Sheepshanks in
the Volume, *morocco, uncut, top edge gilt*
1111 Shelley (P. B.) Poetical Works, edited by H. B. Forman,
2 vol. *portrait and frontispiece, blue morocco extra, gilt
edges*   1882
1112 Sheridan (Rt. Hon. R. B.) Dramatic Works, with Life,
portrait   1867

1113 Shrewsbury (Earl) On the Estatica of Caldaro and the Addolorata of Capriana, *half morocco*, 1842—Trench (T.) Notes from past Life (1818-32), *Oxford*, 1862—Letters from Cambridge, 1828—Everett (W.) on the Cam, 1866 —Whytehead (T.) College Life, *Cambridge*, 1845— Clark (E. C.) Cambridge Legal Studies, *ib.* 1888   (6)

1114 Sidonii Apollinaris Opera Latine avec une Etude sur Sidoine par E. Baret, *half gilt vellum*   *Paris*, 1879

1115 Sigeberti Gemblacensis Monachi Opera Omnia. Accedunt Chronicon Polonorum et aliorum Fragmenta, *calf gilt*   *ib.* 1854

1116 Silvester (Bernardus) de Mundi Universitate edentibus C. S. Barach et J. Wrobel   *Insbruck*, 1876

1117 Simeon (C.) Life, select Writings and Correspondence, edited by Rev. W. Carus, *portrait*   1847

1118 Smith (J. J.) Catalogue of Manuscripts in Gonville and Caius College Library, *Cambridge*, 1849—Cranwell (E.) Index of English Books printed before 1600, in Trinity College Library, *view, ib.* 1847—Collett (W. R.) List of Early Printed Books in Gonville and Caius College Library, *ib.* 1850   (3)

1119 Smith (Rev. Sydney) Works, 3 vol. *portrait, with portrait from Fraser's Magazine added*   1845

1120 Smith (W.) Dictionary of Greek and Roman Antiquities, *numerous woodcuts*   1842

1121 Smith (W.) Dictionary of Greek and Roman Biography, 3 vol. *numerous woodcuts*   1844-49

1122 Smith (W.) Dictionary of Greek and Roman Geography, 2 vol. *numerous woodcuts*   1854-57

1123 Smith (W.) Dictionary of the Bible, 3 vol. *numerous woodcuts*, 1860-63—Dictionary of Christian Antiquities, being a continuation of the Dictionary of the Bible, edited by W. Smith and S. Cheetham, 2 vol. *numerous woodcuts*, 1875-80   *5 vol.*

1124 Smyth (Prof. W.) Lectures on Modern History, 2 vol. *Cambridge*, 1840—Lectures on the French Revolution, 3 vol. 1842   *5 vol.*

1125 SOPHOCLIS TRAGŒDIÆ, Græce, FIRST EDITION, *autograph signature and MS. Notes of* " Johannes Baldwinus," *red morocco, gilt edges*   *Venetiis, Aldus*, 1502

. Very scarce.   Sir J. Thorold's copy sold for £12.

1126 Sophocles Ajax, as represented at Cambridge with English Translation by R. C. Jebb, *very rare, Cambridge*, 1882

1127 Sophocles Œdipus Tyrannus, Œdipus Coloneus, Antigone and Philoctetes in Greek with Notes, Commentary and English Prose Translation by R. C. Jebb, 4 vol. *Cambridge*, 1883-90

G 2

1128 Sophocles Tragedies, in English Verse, by Rev. T. Dale, 2 vol. in 1   1824

1129 Sophoclis Tragœdiæ, Græce cum Notis Variorum curante T. Gaisford, 2 vol. *Oxonii*, 1826—Scholia in Sophoclem Græce e Cod. MS. Laurentiano descripsit P. Elmsley, *ib.* 1825—Beatson (B. W.) Index Græcitatis Sophocleæ, *Cantab.* 1830, *calf extra*   4 *vol.*

1130 Southey (R.) Life of Wesley, 2 vol. *portraits, calf gilt* 1820

1131 Southey (R.) Poetical Works, 10 vol. *portrait and views* 1838

1132 Southey (R.) The Doctor, *portrait and view, autograph letter of A. J. Mayor respecting Mr. Luard choosing a book in Memory of J. Grote*   1848

1133 Southey (R.) Life of Nelson, 1830—Sketches of Venetian History, 2 vol. 1838—Hollings (J. F.) Life of Gustavus Adolphus, *portrait*, 1838—Schiller (F.) Thirty Years' War ; Trials of Counts Egmond and Horn, 2 vol. *portraits, calf extra, Edinb.* 1828—Lane (E. W.) Modern Egyptians, 3 vol. 1846—Markham (Mrs.) Malta and Poland, *map*, 1836—Brewster (Sir D.) Life of Sir Is. Newton, *portrait, calf extra*, 1831—Tytler (P. F.) Life of Sir Walter Raleigh, *portraits, seals and autographs, Edinb.* 1833   (12)

1134 Spence (J.) Anecdotes, with Notes and Life by S. W. Singer, *portrait, calf extra, uncut, top edge gilt*   1820

1135 Spenser (E.) Works, *portrait and vignette title, with a MS. Poem of* 18 *lines each ending in ive, dated March* 18, 1862, *morocco, gilt edges*   1856

1136 Spinckes (N.) Devotions, *red morocco extra, gilt edges Oxford*, 1841

1137 Spirit of Public Journals from 1797 to 1806 inclusive, 10 vol. 1797-1807, and for 1811   11 *vol.*

1138 Staal (Madame de) Œuvres, 2 vol. *gilt vellum, with arms of John Earl of Clare in gold on sides*   *Paris*, 1821

1139 Stanton (V. H.) Jewish and Christian Messiah, *Edinb.* 1886

1140 Stanley (Dean A. P.) Historical Memorials of Westminster Abbey, with Supplement, 2 vol. *plates, with autograph letter of the author added, cloth, uncut*   1868-69

1141 Statii Opera cum Orthographia et Flexu Dictionum Græcarum, *calf*   *Venetiis, Aldus*, 1519
  *** Scarce. Sir J. Thorold's copy sold for £3 3s.

1142 Stendhal (M. de, Henry Beyle) Promenades dans Rome, 2 vol. *half vellum, Paris*, 1873—Beaumont (G. de) L'Irland sociale, politique et religieuse, 2 vol. *ib.* 1881 —Ampère (J. J.) La Grèce, Rome et Dante, *half vellum, ib.* 1870—Thierry (A.) Derniers Temps de l'Empire d'Occident, *half vellum, ib.* 1867   (6)

1143 Stephen (L.) Life of H. Fawcett, 2 *portraits*, 1885—
Sketches of Cambridge by a Don, 1865—Swift, 1882 (3)

1144 Stephen (L.) and S. Lee, Dictionary of National Biography (Abbadie to Hindley), 26 vol. *with autograph
letter of L. Stephen added, half morocco extra*, 1885-91

1145 Sterne (L.) Tristram Shandy and Sentimental Journey,
2 vol. *portrait, half calf extra, Leipzig*, 1849-61—Post-
humous Works (by R. Griffiths), 2 vol. *calf*, 1770 (4)

1146 Stillingfleet (Bp. E.) Origines Britanicæ, 2 vol. *calf gilt,
Oxford*, 1842—Origines Sacræ, 2 vol. *calf extra, ib.* 1836

1147 Stirling-Maxwell (Sir W.) Don John of Austria, 2 vol.
LARGE PAPER, *numerous wood-engravings, ornamented
cloth, uncut* 1883

1148 STOBÆI (JOANNIS) FLORILEGIUM, Græce, et Latino
Carmine redditum ab Hugone Grotio, edidit T. Gaisford,
4 vol. *with autograph letter of T. Gaisford added, blue
morocco extra, gilt edges, Oxonii*, 1822 — ECLOGÆ
PHYSICÆ ET ETHICÆ. Accedit Hieroclis Commentarius
in aurea Carmina Pythagoriorum, ad MSS. Codd.
recensuit T. Gaisford, 2 vol. *blue morocco extra, uncut,
top edge gilt, ib.* 1850, LARGE PAPER 6 *vol.*

₊ Only 25 copies printed, and now very scarce. Williams's
copy sold for £12 12s.

1149 Strickland (Agnes) Lives of the Queens of England,
12 vol. *portraits and vignette titles, uncut* 1842-48

1150 Stubbs (W.) Select Charters and other Illustrations of
English Constitutional History, *Oxford*, 1870—Smith
(J. G.) Diocesan Histories, Worcester, *map*, 1883—
Tytler (P. F.) Life of Henry VIII, *portrait, calf extra,
Edinb.*1837—Jessopp (A.) Diocesan Histories, Norwich,
map, with author's autograph inscription, 1884—Hutton
(W. H.) Misrule of Henry III, *cuts*, 1887 (5)

1151 Sunday Library. Yonge (Charlotte Mary) Pupils of St.
John the Evangelist, 1868—Kingsley (C.) The Hermits
(1868)—Guizot (M.) Great Christians of France, St.
Louis and Calvin (1868), 3 vol. *frontispieces and vignette titles, half calf gilt*, 1868—Oliphant (Mrs.) Francis
of Assisi, *frontispieces and vignette title*, 1868—Martin
(Frances) Angelique Arnauld, 1869 5 *vol.*

1152 SURTEES SOCIETY'S PUBLICATIONS, a set, 86 vol. *uncut*
1835-90

1153 Swainson (C. A.) Nicene and Apostles Creed, with
Account of the Athanasian Creed, *facsimile* 1875

1154 Swetchine (Madame) Sa Vie et ses Œuvres publiées par
le Comte de Falloux, 2 vol. *half red morocco, uncut, top
edges gilt* *Paris,* 1863

1155 Swift (Dean J.) Works, 21 vol. *calf* 1751-67

1156 Symonis Simeonis et Willelmi de Worcestre Itineraria quibus accedit Tractatus de Metro edente J. Nasmith, *blue morocco extra, leather joints, gilt edges*
Cantabrigiæ, 1778

1157 Taciti Opera cum Notis G. Brotier, curante A. J. Valpy, 5 vol. LARGE PAPER, *calf extra, gilt edges* 1812
₊ Presentation copy to Dr. Valpy of Reading.

1158 Tacitus ab Im. Bekkero recognitus, 2 vol. *calf extra*
Lipsiæ, 1831

1159 Tales from Blackwood, 12 vol. *cloth* *Edinb. n. d.*

1160 Talfourd (Sir T. N.) Tragedies, Sonnets and Verses, *half russia extra*, 1844—Scott (Sir W.) Lord of the Isles and Miscellaneous Poems, *Edinb.* 1836—Byron (Lord) Poems, 1833—Goldsmith (O.) Poems, 1836—Gray (T.) Poems, 1837—Herrick (R.) Hesperides, 2 vol. *morocco, gilt edges*, 1844 ; and 5 others, Poetical (12)

1161 Taylor (C.) Teaching of the Twelve Apostles, with Illustrations from the Talmud, *Camb.* 1886 — Maurice (Priscilla) Help for Sick Poor, and Prayers for the Sick and Dying, 2 vol. 1863-64—Marriott (C.) Hints on Private Devotion, *Oxford*, 1848 ; and 8 others, Religious (12)

1162 Taylor (Bp. J.) Whole Works, with Life by Bp. R. Heber, revised by Rev. C. P. Eden, 10 vol. *portrait, red morocco extra, gilt edges* 1850-54

1163 Teesdale (Mrs. M.) Poems, edited by her Children for private circulation, *portrait, and views with elegant head and tail pieces, presentation copy with Edmund Teesdale's autograph inscription, cloth, gilt edges* *Edinb.* 1888

1164 Tennyson (A. Lord) Poems, *portrait and illustrations by Creswick, Millais, Mulready, Maclise, C. Stanfield, Horsley, &c. ornamented cloth, gilt edges* 1862

1165 Tennyson (A. Lord) Poetical Works, 8 vol. *ports.* 1888

1166 Tennyson (A. Lord) Lover's Tale, 1879—Maud and other Poems, 1855—The Princess, 1850—Demeter and other Poems, 1889—Ode on the Duke of Wellington, 1852 (5)

1167 Terentii Comœdiæ cum Notis Variorum, *autograph of Wm. Prince of Orange, and a Note in Porson's handwriting, vellum* *Lugd. Bat.* 1651

1168 Testamentum Novum, Græce, 2 vol. *O mirificam Edition, old French red morocco, gilt edges*
Lutetiæ, R. Stephanus, 1546
₊ Scarce. The Wodhull copy sold for £1 11s.

1169 Testamentum Novum, Græce, LARGE PAPER, *old black morocco, gold tooling, gilt edges* *Cantab. T. Buck*, 1632

1170 Testamentum Novum Græce cum Commentatione isago-
gica edidit A. F. C. Tischendorf, 2 vol. in 1, *Lipsiæ*,
1759—Evangelia Apocrypha, Gr. et Lat. edidit C. Tischendorf, *ib.* 1853 —Apocalypses Apocryphæ Mosis,
Esdræ, Pauli, Johannis, item Mariæ Dormitio Gr.
curante C. Tischendorf, *ib.* 1766, *gilt vellum*   3 *vol.*

1171 Testamenta XII Patriarcharum Græce edita, with Dissertation thereon by R. Sinker   *Cambridge*, 1869

1172 Testament (New) in Greek and English, LARGE PAPER,
morocco, gilt edges   *S. Baxter & Sons, n. d.*

1173 Testament (New) Greek, Text revised by Bp. B. F. West-
cott and F. J. A. Hort, 2 vol. *Camb.* 1881 — Westcott
(Bp. B. F.) Revelation of the risen Lord, *ib.* 1881—
Westcott (Bp. B. F.) Introduction to the Study of the
Gospels, *autograph letter of author added, ib.* 1860—
Hort (F. J. A.) Sermon at the Consecration of Bp.
Westcott, 1890   (5)

1174 Testament (New) translated, with Notes, by G. Wakefield, 3 vol. *uncut*   1791

1175 Testament (New) in Greek, with Prolegomena and Commentary by Dean H. Alford, 4 vol. in 5, *uncut*, 1849-61

1176 Testament (Neue) *morocco, gilt edges, S. Bagster, s. a.—*
Allegemeine Gebetbuch von England übersetzt von J.
H. W. Küper, 1823—Blüthen Christlicher Dichtung,
frontispiece, cloth, gilt edges, Stuttgart, 1866—Württem-
berg Gesangbuch, *frontispiece, stamped calf, gilt edges,
in case, ib.* 1852—Neale (J. M.) Hymni Ecclesiæ e
Breviariis et Missalibus, *Oxonii,* 1851—Thring (G.)
Church of England Hymn Book, 1882—Thring (G.)
Hymns and Sacred Lyrics, 1874; and 5, Religious (12)

1177 THACKERAY (W. M.) THE SNOB, *Cambridge,* 1829—THE
GOWNSMAN, *ib.* 1830 — Cambridge Odes by Peter Per-
sius, *ib. n. d.*—Snobs' Trip to Paris, *ib. n. d.*—Progress
to B. A. *ib.* 1830 — The Individual, 15 Nos. *on coloured
papers, ib.* 1886-37, *uncut, extremely rare*   *in* 1 *vol*

1178 Thackeray (W. M.) Pendennis, 2 vol. FIRST EDITION,
illustrations by the author, cloth, uncut   1849-50

  *** With facsimile photo of extra illustration :—" Arrival of
Doctor Doddridge in Heaven," "Shew me to my bed-
room my good woman." Also shewing sketch by
Thackeray on flap of envelope in which the original of
this was sent to Dr. Thompson, late Master of Trinity
College. Only four copies were taken and the negative
has since been destroyed.

1179 Thackeray (W. M.) Henry Esmond, 3 vol. FIRST EDITION,
half morocco   1852

1180 Thackeray (W. M.) Christmas Books. Mrs. Perkins's Ball; Our Street and Dr. Birch, *illustrations by the author,* 1857
1181 Thackeray (W. M.) Ballads, *portrait and beautiful illustrations by the author, Mrs. Butler (Miss E. Thompson), G. Du Maurier, J. Collier, &c. ornamental cloth, g.e.* 1879
1182 Thackeray (W. M.) Ballads, 1856 — Shabby Genteel Story, 1857— Fitz-Boodle Papers and Men's Wives, 1857—Fatal Boots and Cox's Diary, 1855, *in the original covers* (5)
1183 Thackeray (W. M.) English Humourists of the XVIIIth Century, 1853—Miscellanies, vol. II, 1856—Barry Lyndon, *half calf extra,* 1856 — The Newcomes, 4 vol. in 2, *half calf extra, Leipzig,* 1854-55 ; and 2 others (7)
1184 Thackeray (W. M.) Vanity Fair, 2 vol. 1867 — Burlesques, 1869—Irish Sketch Book and Journey from Cornhill to Grand Cairo, 1869 — Paris Sketch Book and Memoirs of C. J. Yellowplush, 1868—Catherine, Little Travels, Fitz-Boodle Papers, &c. 1869, *portrait and plates* 6 *vol.*
1185 Thiele (C. G. G.) Genesis et Prophetæ Minores Hebraice, 2 vol. *Lipsiæ,* 1847-51 — Arnold (T. K.) First Hebrew Book, 1851—Bernard (H. H.) Guide to the Hebrew Student, 1839 (4)
1186 Theocriti Idyllia cum Scholiis, Græce, Cura Z. Calliergi, *russia, gilt edges* *Romæ,* 1516
   *** " Edition rare et recherchée, vendue 73 francs De Cotte."—*Brunet.*
1187 Theocriti Eidyllia, Græce Latinis pleraque Numeris a C. A. Wetstenio reddita cum Notis L. C. Valckenaer, *autograph and MS. Notes of Bp. C. J. Blomfield, uncut* *Lugd. Bat.* 1773
1188 Theocritus Græce recensente C. Wordsworth, *with autograph letter of editor added, half morocco, uncut, top edge gilt* *Cantab.* 1844
1189 Theophrasti Characteres, Gr. et Lat. cum Notis Variorum et P. Needham, LARGE PAPER, *fine copy in old calf* *ib.* 1712
   *** Scarce. Dent's copy sold for £4 5s.
1190 Theophrastus Characters, in Greek and English, by R. C. Jebb, *with autograph letters of R. C. Jebb and E. Atkinson, respecting the meaning of Enchiridion, added, Camb.* 1870
1191 Thierry (A.) Histoire de la Conquête de l'Angleterre par les Normands, 4 vol. *Paris,* 1846 — Récits des Temps Mérovingiens, 2 vol. *ib.* 1867, *half calf gilt* 6 *vol.*
1192 Thiers (A.) Histoire de la Révolution Française, 2 vol. *map, portraits and plates, half red morocco extra* *Bruxelles,* 1840
1193 Thirlwall (Bp. C.) History of Greece, 8 vol. *maps,* 1845-52

1194 Thoms (W. J.) Early English Prose Romances, 3 vol.
half Roxburghe, uncut 1858
1195 Thomson (J.) Works, 4 vol. *portrait and plates, calf,* 1773
1196 Thomson (R.) Chronicles of London Bridge, LARGE
PAPER, *woodcuts, half morocco, uncut, top edge gilt,* 1827
1197 Thomson (R.) Historical Essay on the Magna Charta of
King John, with Great Charter in Latin and English,
the Charters of Liberties and Confirmations, Charter of
the Forests and other Instruments connected with them,
LARGE PAPER, *woodcuts, cloth, uncut* 1829
1198 Thring (E.) Education and School, *Cambridge,* 1867—
On the Principles of Grammar, *Oxford,* 1868—Exercises in grammatical Analysis, *ib.* 1868—Latin Gradual,
Camb. 1871—Construing Book, *ib.* 1855 (5)
1199 Thucydides, Græce et Latine, edente P. Elmsley, 6 vol.
half russia extra *Edinb. G. Laing,* 1804
1200 Thucydides in Greek, with Notes by T. Arnold, 3 vol.
maps, calf gilt *Oxford,* 1830-35
1201 Tigri (G.) Canti Popolari Toscani, *Firenze,* 1869—
Leopardi (G.) Poesie, *Milano,* 1878—Leopardi (G.)
Operette morali, *vellum, Livorno,* 1870—Preti (G.)
Poesie, *Bologna,* 1644—Solazzi (E.) Letteratura Inglese,
Milano, 1879—Goldoni (C.) Commedie scelte, *calf
extra, Parigi,* 1841—Casti (G. B.) Gli Animali par-
lanti, *frontispiece and vignette title, calf extra,* 1822 (7)
1202 Tilley (A.) Literature of the French Renaissance, *author's
autograph inscription, Cambridge,* 1885—Merryweather
(F. S.) Bibliomania in the Middle Ages, 1849—Catalogue of Lichfield Cathedral Library, 1888—Clark (A.)
Cataloguing of MSS. in the Bodleian Library, *Oxford,*
1890—Macmillan and Bowes Catalogues of Cambridge
Books, *n. d.*—Catalogue of Grosvenor Gallery Library,
1883 ; and 4 other Catalogues (10)
1203 Todhunter (I.) William Whewell. An Account of his
Writings with Selections from his Correspondence, 2 vol.
1876—Algebra, *Cambridge,* 1858 ; and 6 other Mathematical Works of Todhunter (9)
1204 Topham (E.) Life of J. Elwes (Miser), *portrait and
pedigree, calf,* 1790—Lackington (J. *Bookseller*) Life,
portrait, 1791—Evelyn (J.) Diary, *n. d.* (3)
1205 Toulgoët (E. De) Les Musées de Rome avec une Etude
sur l'Histoire de la Peinture en Italie, *red morocco extra,
leather joints, watered silk linings, gilt edges, with the
Pope's arms in gold on sides* *Paris,* 1867
1206 Toup (J.) Emendationes in Suidam et Hesychium, 4 vol.
russia extra, gilt edges *Oxonii,* 1790
1207 TRACTS FOR THE TIMES, from 1833 to 41, 90 Nos. in
6 vol. *half calf gilt* 1840-41

1208 Treculphi Episcopi Lexoviensis Chronica, *calf, scarce*
           Genevæ, 1597
1209 Trench (Mrs. Richard) Remains, edited by her Son the
  Dean of Westminster, *portrait, cloth, uncut* 1862
1210 Trench (Archbp. R. C.) New Testament Synonyms, 1871
1211 Trench (Archbp. R. C.) Notes on the Parables and
  Miracles of Our Lord, 2 vol. 1855-58—Sacred Latin
  Poetry, 1849   (3)
1212 Trial of Joseph Gerrald for Sedition, *portrait,* 1794—
  Trial of Rev. T. S. Palmer for Sedition, *Edinb.* 1793—
  King *v.* Lambert and Others for Libel in Morning
  Chronicle, 1794—Horne Tooke's Letter on the reported
  Marriage of the Prince of Wales, 1787, *half russia*
              in 1 *vol.*
1213 Tribute (The), unpublished Poems edited by Lord
  Northampton   1837
 ⁎⁎ Containing first editions of Poems by Lord Tennyson,
  B. Barton, W. Wordsworth, R. Southey, Lord Hough-
  ton, W. S. Landor, &c. &c.

1214 Trollope (Anthony) Last Chronicle of Barset, 2 vol.
  illustrations by G. H. Thomas, half calf gilt 1867
1215 Tryphiodorus Destruction of Troy in English Verse with
  Text in Greek and Latin added, and with Notes by J.
  Meyrick, 2 vol. in 1, LARGE PAPER, *russia extra, leather
  joints, gilt edges, by C. Hering* *Oxford,* 1739-41
 ⁎⁎ This copy sold for £2 in Mr. Beckford's sale.

1216 Tusser (T.) Five hundred Pointes of good Husbandrie
  (in verse), with Introduction, Notes and Glossary by
  W. Payne and S. J. Heritage, *half morocco extra, uncut,
  top edge gilt*   1878
1217 Tyrwhitt (T. *Clerk of the House of Commons*) Proceedings
  and Debates of the House of Commons in 1620-21,
  2 vol. *presentation copy to A. Onslow, with Tyrwhitt's
  autograph letter*   *Oxford,* 1766
1218 Tyrwhitt (T.) Conjecturæ in Æschylum, Euripidem et
  Aristophanem. Accedunt Epistolæ diversorum ad Tyr-
  whittum, *Oxonii,* 1822—Dissertatio de Babrio cum
  Auctario, 1776-81, Orpheus de Lapidibus, Gr. et
  Lat. 1781—Notæ in Toupium, 1790—Conjecturæ in Stra-
  bonem, 1788—Isæi Oratio Gr. 1785—On Passages of
  Shakespeare, *very scarce, Oxford,* 1766, *half morocco,
  uncut, top edges gilt*   *in* 2 *vol.*
1219 Tytler (A. F.) Elements of General History, with Additions and Continuation by E. Nares, 2 vol. *russia extra*
            1831 & 1824
1220 Union Review from January 1863 to December 1875, inclusive, 13 vol. *half calf gilt*   1863-75

1221 Valerii Flacci Argonautica, J. B. Pii Carmen ex quarto
Argonauticon Apollonii, Orphei Argonautica innominato
Interprete, *old French calf, gilt edges*
Venetiis, Aldus, 1523

1222 Valerius Maximus nuper editus, *vellum, gilt gaufré edges*
ib. 1534

⁎⁎ Scarce. Sir John Thorold's copy with dedication damaged
sold for £3 10s.

1223 Vaughan (D. J.) Present Trial of Faith (Leicester
Sermons), 1878 — Thring (E.) Uppingham School
Sermons, *Cambridge,* 1858—Krummacher (F. W.)
Elijah the Tishbite, 1836 (3)

1224 Vaughan (R. A.) Hours with the Mystics, 2 vol. FIRST
EDITION, *uncut, scarce* 1856

1225 Velleius Paterculus cum Notis Variorum curante P. Bur-
manno, *old calf, gilt edges* *Lugd. Bat.* 1719

1226 Ville-Hardouin (Geoffroi de) La Conquête de Constanti-
nople avec la Continuation par Henri de Valenciennes.
Texte original accompagné d'une Traduction par Natalis
de Wailly, *brown morocco extra, gilt edges,* *Paris,* 1872

1227 Villeneuve-Trans (Marquis de) Histoire de Saint Louis
Roi de France, 3 vol. *calf extra* *ib.* 1839

1228 Virgilii Opera cum Notulis illustrabat G. Wakefield,
2 vol. LARGE PAPER, *calf gilt* 1796

1229 Wakefield (G.) Silva critica, 5 vol. in 2, *russia extra*
Cantab. et Lond. 1789-95

1230 Wakefield (G.) Tragediarum Delectus, Hercules Furens,
Alcestis et Ion Euripideæ; Trachiniæ et Philoctetes
Sophocleæ; et Eumenides Æschylea, Græce, 2 vol.
LARGE PAPER, *russia extra, gilt edges* 1794

1231 Wakefield (G.) Memoirs, 2 vol. *portrait, half russia,* 1804

1232 Wakefield (G.) Correspondence with the Rt. Hon. C. J.
Fox, *half russia,* 1813—Observations on Pope, *half calf
gilt,* 1796—Translation of Dio Chrysostom's Select
Essays, *half calf gilt,* 1800 *3 vol.*

1233 Wakefield (G.) Tracts. A Collection of 33 Pamphlets
by Wakefield (*see MS. Lists on fly-leaves*), *mostly rare,
half calf gilt, in* 3 *vol.* 1776-1801

1234 Walbran (J. R.) Guide to Ripon, Fountains Abbey, Har-
rogate, Bolton Priory and Vicinity, *plates* *Ripon,* 1875

1235 Waldegrave (Hon. and Rev. S.) University Sermons, *calf
extra* 1848

1236 Waldstein (C.) Catalogue of Casts in Fitzwilliam Museum, *plate* 1889

1237 Waldstein (C.) Essays on the Art of Pheidias, LARGE
PAPER, *with illustrations, Cambridge,* 1885; and 3 others
by Waldstein (4)

1238 Walpole Earl of Orford (Horace) Catalogue of Royal and Noble Authors, 2 vol. *frontispieces*, 1759—Castle of Otranto, with Life by Lord Dover, *portrait, half calf extra*, 1834 (3)

1239 Wallen (W.) History of Little Maplestead Round Church, *plates* 1836

1240 Walton (W.) Problems of Theoretical Hydrostatics and Hydrodynamics, *Camb.* 1847—Problems of Plane co-ordinate Geometry, *ib.* 1851—Problems of elementary Mechanics, *ib.* 1858—Problems of Theoretical Mechanics, *ib.* 1876, *presentation copies, with Author's autograph inscription, and long holograph letter* 4 *vol.*

1241 Walton (W.) on Differential Calculus, *Camb.* 1845— Pearson (J.) Calculus of finite Differences, *ib.* 1849— Todhunter (I.) Algebra for Beginners, *ib.* 1863—Barrett (A. C.) Mechanics and Hydrostatics, *ib.* 1855— Todhunter (I.) Analytical Geometry of three Dimensions, *ib.* 1858—Bonnycastle (J.) Arithmetic, 1834— Herschell (Sir J. F. W.) Astronomy, *calf extra*, 1833 —Book of Science, Both Series, 2 vol. *woodcuts*, 1833-35 —Wonders of the Heavens, *plates*, 1826 (10)

1242 Ward (W. G.) Ideal of a Christian Church 1844

1243 Warren (S.) Ten Thousand a Year, 3 vol. *Edinb.* 1845— Radcliffe (Ann) The Italian, 2 vol. *Dublin*, 1797— Moore (T.) Epicurean, 1828—French Anas, 3 vol. 1805 (9)

1244 Warton (T.) Poetical Works, with Life by Bp. R. Mant, 2 vol. LARGE PAPER, *portrait, tree-marbled calf extra, uncut, top edges gilt, by Wilson* *Oxford*, 1802

1245 Warton (T.) History of English Poetry, edited by W. C. Hazlitt, 4 *vol.* 1871

1246 Waterloo, Ligny and Quatre Bras Battles, 2 vol. *coloured views, plans, etchings, &c. half calf*, 1817—Cotton (E.) Voice from Waterloo, *portraits and plates, Brussels*, 1847 (3)

1247 Watson (J. S.) Life of Bp. W. Warburton, *portrait*, 1863

1248 Wessenberg (Ign. H.) Die Christlichen Bilder ein Beförderungsmittel des Christlichen Sinnes, 2 vol. *frontispieces and plates, half calf* *Constanz*, 1827

1249 Wetherell (E.) Wide, Wide World, *n. d.*—Searle (E.) Friends and Neighbours, *frontispiece*, 1872—Stretton (H.) Wonderful Life, *front.* 1875 ; and others (10)

1250 Wharton (H.) Historia de Episcopis et Decanis Londinensibus necnon Assavensibus, *half morocco, t. e.g.* 1695

1251 Whewell (W.) Sermons on the Foundation of Morals, *Cambridge*, 1837 ; and other sermons in the Volume, *half calf gilt*

1252 Whewell (W.) Plurality of Worlds, *frontispiece*, 1854—
Kingsley (C.) Phaethon, *Camb.* 1852 — Thackeray
(S. W.) Land and Community, 1889—Hutton (J.) Deaf-
and-Dumb Land, *plates, n. d.* (4)

1253 Whewell (W.) Architectural Notes on German Churches,
plates, autograph letter of author added, Cambridge, 1842

1254 Whibley (C.) In Cap and Gown. Three Centuries of
Cambridge Wit, 1889—Cambridge Trifles, 1881—
Sketches of Cantabs, 2 *illustrations by H. K. Browne,*
1850—The Sizar, *Camb.* 1799 (4)

1255 Whiston (W.) Memoirs and Liturgy, 2 vol. *half vellum*
1749-50

1256 White (G.) Natural History of Selborne, &c. *plates, calf
extra,* 1834—D'Israeli (I.) Curiosities of Literature,
half calf gilt, 1866—Walcott (M.) Minsters and Abbey
Ruins, 1860—Ripa (Father) China and West Indies, by
M. G. Lewis, 2 vol. in 1, 1844-45 (4)

1257 Wigram (W. K.) Justices' Note-Book, *author's autograph
inscription* 1881

1258 Williams (G.) The Holy City (Jerusalem), 2 vol. *plates,
with autograph letter of the author added, calf extra,* 1849

1259 Williams (G.) Orthodox Church of the East in the
XVIIIth Century, *portrait of the Patriarch, Cambridge,*
1868—Pearson (J. B.) Chaplains to the Levant Com-
pany, *ib.* 1883—Littledale (R. F.) Council of Trent,
1888—Oakeley (F.) on the Tractarian Movement, 1865
—Brewer (J. S.) Athanasian Creed vindicated and its
Origin, 2 vol. 1871-72 ; and 8 others, Religious (14)

1260 Williams (I.) The Cathedral, *plates, Oxford,* 1841—
Evangelical Melodies, 1849—Lyra Innocentium, *Oxford,*
1846—Neale (J. M.) Sequentiæ ex Missalibus, *calf gilt,*
1852—Williams (I.) Hymns translated from the Parisian
Breviary, 1839—Lyra Apostolica, *Derby,* 1841 ; and 10
others, Religious (16)

1261 Willis (R.) Remarks on the Architecture of the Middle
Ages especially of Italy, *plates, autograph letter of author
added, cloth, uncut* *Cambridge,* 1835

1262 Willis (R.) Architectural Histories of York and Worcester Cathedrals, Sherborne Minster and Glastonbury
Abbey, in 1 vol. *plates, half calf gilt, with author's autograph inscriptions* 1848-63-65-66

1263 Willis (R.) History of the Monastery of Christ Church,
Canterbury, *plates, author's autograph letter added,* 1869

1264 Wilson (J.) Memorabilia Cantabrigiæ, *views of colleges
and portraits of the founders* 1803

1265 Wilson (Professor J.) Noctes Ambrosianæ, 4 vol.
Edinb. 1855-56

1266 Wodhull (M.) Poems, *portrait, presentation copy to Sir R. P. Jodrell, with author's autograph inscription, half morocco, uncut, top edge gilt* 1804

*** Privately printed for presents only.

1267 Wood (W.) Index Testaceologicus, or Catalogue of Shells, *38 coloured plates, half russia, uncut* 1825

1268 Woodford (Bp. J. R.) Three Ely Charges, *Cambridge,* 1877-81-85—Lightfoot (Bp. J. B.) Durham Charge, 1882—Douglas (Bp. H. A.) Bombay Charge, *Bombay,* 1875, *half calf gilt in 1 vol.*

1269 Wordsworth (C.) Athens and Attica, *maps and plates, King's College prize, calf extra, gilt edges, with arms in gold on sides* 1837

1270 Wordsworth (C.) Tour in Italy, 2 vol. 1863

1271 Wordsworth (C.) Social Life at the English Universities in the XVIIIth Century, *with autograph letter from the author containing corrections Cambridge,* 1874

1272 Wordsworth (W.) Poetical Works, *portrait and vignette title* 1847

1273 Wordsworth (W.) Poetical Works, 6 vol. 1865

1274 Wordsworth (W.) Poetical Works, *portrait and plates Edinb. n. d.*

1275 Worsley (T.) Province of the Intellect in Religion, *author's autograph inscription, calf extra,* 1845—Christian Drift of Cambridge Work, *author's autograph letter, cloth, Cambridge,* 1865 (2)

1276 Worsley (T.) Order and Method of the Bible, *charts, with photograph portrait added, calf gilt* 1887

*** Presentation copy from Sir W. C. Worsley, by whom the work was printed for private circulation only.

1277 Wraxall (Sir N.) Memoirs of the Kings of France of the Race of Valois, 2 vol. *calf gilt* 1777

1278 Wraxall (Sir N.) Historical Memoirs of my own Time, 2 vol. *portrait, calf extra* 1815

1279 Wright (W. A.) Bible Word-book, *with author's autograph inscription, Cambridge,* 1884—Apocryphal Scriptures, with Notes and Introduction by Rev. W. R. Churton, 1884—Westcott (B. F.) Historic Faith and Social Aspects of Christianity, 2 vol. 1883-87 (4)

1280 Wright (T.) Biographia Britannica Literaria, Anglo-Saxon and Anglo-Norman periods, 2 vol. 1842-46

1281 Yonge (Charlotte Mary) Musings over the Christian Year and Lyra Innocentium, with Recollections of the Rev. J. Keble, *Oxford,* 1871—Book of Golden Deeds, 1876 (2)

1282 Yonge (C. M.) Novels, viz. Heir of Radcliffe, Heartsease, Dynevor Terrace, Daisy Chain, Hopes and Fears, Young Stepmother, The Trial, Danvers Papers and Prince and Page, and Caged Lion, 17 vol. in 9, *half calf extra*
Leipzig, 1855-70

1283 Young (Sir C. G. *Garter*) Catalogue of the Arundel Manuscripts in the Library of the College of Arms
1829

⁎ Only 35 copies printed for private distribution. Dr. Bliss's copy sold for £1 18s.

1284 XENOPHONTIS OPERA OMNIA, Gr. et Lat. cum Chronologia Xenophontea Dodwelli et quatuor Tabulis Geographicis, edidit E. Wells, 5 vol. in 9, LARGE PAPER, *portrait, frontispieces and maps, title page of vol. IV inlaid, very fine copy, presented to Andrew Fountain by the editor, with his autograph inscription, in old gilt calf*
Oxonii, 1693-1703

⁎ To obtain a Large Paper copy of Wells's Xenophon, which has always been considered the rarest work issued from the Oxford Press, collectors of rarities have considered almost impossible. Count Macarthy's copy, wanting portrait and several sheets, sold for 1,520 francs; Sir M. Sykes's, wanting vol. II, for £26 5s.; and Viscount Hampden's, wanting first part of vol. V, for £158 11s. To form a perfect copy, the Rev. T. Williams purchased all three (MacCarthy, Sykes and Hampden), and his own imperfect set, had them bound, costing him together £320. This copy is much finer than that in the Grenville Library.

QUARTO.

1285 Rye (W.) Carrow Abbey, *plates, half vellum, uncut*
Norwich, 1889

1286 Saunders (F.) Story of some famous Books, LARGE PAPER, *half morocco, uncut, top edge gilt* 1887

1287 Scharf (G.) Description of the Diptych at Wilton House, containing a Portrait of Richard II, *plates*
printed for the Arundel Society, 1882

1288 Simplicii Commentarius in Enchiridion Epicteti, Gr. et Lat. cum Notis C. Salmasii, *Lugd. Bat.* 1640—Cebetis Tabula, Gr. Arab. et Lat. Item Aurea Carmina Pythagoræ cum Paraphrasi Arabica J. Elichmanni et Præfatione C. Salmasii, *ib.* 1640, *old olive morocco, borders of gold, gilt edges, with arms within a wreath in gold on sides*
in 1 *vol.*

1289 Small (J.) English metrical Homilies from Manuscripts of the XIVth Century, with Introduction and Notes, *facsimile* *Edinb.* 1862

1290 Smith (R. P.) Early Writings, with a few Verses in later Years, edited by his surviving Son, R. V. F. (*Rt. Hon. R. Vernon Smith, M.P. for Northampton*) *half morocco, uncut* 1850

∗ Only a few copies printed for presents.

1291 Sophoclis Scholia, Græce, *old red morocco, gilt gaufré edges* In Gymnasio Mediceo Caballini Montis *i.e. Romæ Typis Z. Calliergi*, 1518

∗ First and rarest edition. Hibbert's copy sold for £1 16s.

1292 Statii Silvæ cum Notis J. Marklandi, *old gilt calf*, 1728

1293 Stobæi (Joannis) Collectiones Sententiarum, Græce, *Bp. C. J. Blomfield's copy, with his book-plate, russia, gilt edges, Venetiis*, 1535-36—Duporti (J.) Homeri Gnomologia, *Cantab.* 1660—Sallustii Opera cum Notis Variorum et J. Wasse, *ib.* 1710 (3)

1294 Stubbs (W.) Registrum Sacrum Anglicanum, or Course of Episcopal Succession in England, *half vellum* Oxford, 1858

1295 Stukeley (W.) Palæographia Britannica (Origines Roystonianæ), *plates*, 1743—Parkin (C.) Answer to Stukeley, *plates*, 1744, *half calf gilt* in 1 vol.

1296 Suetonii Opera et in illa Commentarius S. Pitisci, 2 vol. LARGE PAPER, *plates by Luykens, old tree marbled calf* Leovardiæ, 1714-15

1297 Tacchini (P.) Passaggio di Venere sul Sole 8-9 Decembre 1874 osservato a Muddapur nel Bengala, *coloured plates* Palermo, 1875

1298 Tacito, Lat. et Ital. volgarizzato da L. Valeriani, 5 vol. LARGE PAPER, *portraits, vellum, uncut, Firenze*, 1818-20

1299 Taylor (J.) de inope Debitore in Partis dissecando. Accedunt Notæ ad Marmor Bosporanum, de Voce Yonane, Explicatio Inscriptionis in antiquo Marmore Oxon et Directions for the Study of English History and Antiquities, *Cantab.* 1742—Marmor Sandvicense cum Commentario et Notis, *ib.* 1743 (2)

1300 Testament (New), in Greek, after Scholz, with six important English Translations (Wiclif's, Tyndale's, Cranmer's, Genevan, Anglo-Rhemish and Authorized), or English Hexapla Edition, preceded by an historical Account of the English Translations, *autograph letter of E. Kirwan added, calf extra* 1841

1301 Testament (New), in Greek, with Latin Version of Jerome. The Prolegomena, by S. P. Tregelles, 1857-79

1302 Testamento (Nuovo) volgarizzato (con Testo Latino) ed esposte in Note da C. M. Curci, 3 vol. *half vellum* Napoli, 1879-86

1303 Thackeray (F. St. John) Eton College Library, *photographic view* Eton, 1881

1304 Theocriti Quæ supersunt cum Scholiis, Græce cum Notis Variorum et J. Toupii, edidit T. Warton, *old calf*
Oxonii, 1770
1305 Theophrasti Characteres Gr. recensente J. Wilkes, *calf, gilt edges* 1790
1306 Thomæ de Aquino Summa de Articulis Fidei et Ecclesiæ Sacramentis, *fine copy in green morocco extra, borders of gold, tooled leather joints, gilt edges, by Schefer, with arms of Gomez de la Cortina, in gold on sides*
s. l. & a. sed Coloniæ, Ulricus Zell, circa 1467
1307 Tomkins (J. C.) Memoir of Cosmo Innes, *autograph letter of author added* *Edinb.* 1874
1308 Tomlins (Sir T. E.) Law-Dictionary, 2 vol. *old calf, backs broken* 1820
1309 Topographical Miscellanies, *plates, half calf gilt* 1792
1310 Translations into Latin and Greek Verse, *Cambridge*, 1884
1311 Trump (J.) Manuale pro Conficiendis Processibus, *half vellum* *Neapoli*, 1876
1312 Tweddell (J.) Remains (Letters, Prolusiones Juveniles, &c.) *portrait and plates, half bound* 1815
1313 Tyrwhitt (T.) Epistle to Florio at Oxford, FIRST EDITION, *half morocco, uncut, top edge gilt, scarce* 1749
1314 Vasari (G.) Vite de' più eccellenti Pittori, Scultori ed Architetti, 7 vol. (wanting vol. VI), *portraits, uncut*
Firenze, 1770-72
1315 Virgilii Opera perpetua Adnotatione illustrata a C. G. Heyne. (Recognovit R. Porson), 8 parts in 4 vol. LARGEST PAPER, *vignettes, fine copy in gilt russia, by Baumgarten, with Wodhull arms in gold on sides*, 1793
₊ Only a few copies printed for subscribers at £21. Stevens's copy sold for £16 16s.
1316 Virgille ses Faitz merveilleux, black letter, *facsimile reprinted on vellum, half morocco, t. e. g. Paris, G. Nywerd, s. d.*
1317 Virgilio L'Eneide tradotta da A. Caro, *illustrations by Raphael, Poussin, Guido Reni, &c.* *Milano*, 1879
1318 Vivaldi de Monte Regali (J. L.) Opus Regale, *woodcuts, russia extra* *Lugduni*, 1508
1319 Walcott (M. E. C.) Scoti-Monasticon; the Ancient Church of Scotland, *map, ground plans and views, morocco extra, uncut* 1874
1320 Walpole, Earl of Orford (Horace) Historic Doubts on the Life and Reign of Richard III, *portrait*, 1768— Supplement, edited by Dr. E. C. Hawtrey, *n. d. old red morocco, borders of gold, gilt edges* *in 1 vol.*
1321 Walpole (F. Henry, S. J. *executed at York, 17 April*, 1595) Letters, with Notes by A. Jessopp, *facsimile, morocco extra, gilt edges* *Norwich*, 1873
₊ Only 50 copies printed for private circulation.

H

1322 Walter of Henley's Husbandry, with an anonymous Husbandry, Senechancie and Robert Grosseteste's Rules, Transcripts, Translations and Glossary by Elizabeth Lamond 1890

1323 Westwood (J. O.) Palæographia Sacra Pictoria, *numerous illustrations, illuminated in gold and colours, of ancient versions of the Bible copied from illuminated Manuscripts, half morocco, uncut, top edge gilt* 1843-45

1324 Whewell (W.) Ellegiacks, *privately printed and rare, Camb.* 1856— Whytehead's Installation Ode, *ib.* 1842— Wordsworth (W.) Installation Ode, *ib.* 1847—Neale (J. M.) Songs and Ballads, 1844 ; and other Poems, in the Volume, *half morocco, uncut, top edge gilt*

1325 Whewell (W.) Second Memoir on the fundamental Antithesis of Philosophy, *Cambridge*, 1848 ; other Tracts by Whewell, Donaldson, Munro and Thomson, and including privately printed Life of W. Martin Leake and F. Field's Otium Norvicense, part I, in the volume, *half calf gilt*

1326 Willoughby (Lady) Diary, 2 vol. *half calf extra, uncut, top edges gilt* 1844-48

1327 [Wolcot (J.)] Bozzi and Piozzi, by Peter Pindar, *frontispiece, half calf gilt* 1786

1328 Wordsworth (W.) Sonnet on Rebuilding St. Mary's Church, Cardiff, *facsimiled*, 1842—Butler (H. M.) Crossing the Bar, and a few other Translations, with Hymn on the Death of the Young, with Latin Translation, *Cambridge*, 1890—Gray (T.) Elegy in English and Latin, by H. A. J. Munro, *ib. n. d.* (4)

1329 Wornum (R. N.) Hans Holbein and the Meier Madonna, *plates* *printed for the Arundel Society*, 1871

1330 Wright (A.) Court Hand restored, *plates* 1879

1331 Wyatt (Sir M. Digby) Notices of Sculpture in Ivory with Catalogue of Specimens by E. Oldfield, 9 *photographs* 1856

1332 Xenophontis Cyri Anabasis Gr. et Lat. cum Notis T Hutchinson, *map, russia extra* *Cantab.* 1785

1333 Yates (R.) History of St. Edmund's Bury, LARGE PAPER, *views by W. Yates, russia extra* 1805

1334 Yates (Richard) History of St. Edmund's Bury, with Additions, *views by W. Yates* (14 *additional*), *uncut,* 1843

1335 Young (J.) Catalogues of the Pictures at Grosvenor House, at Leigh Court, of J. J. Angerstein, and of Sir J. F. Leicester, Bart. 4 vol. *with etchings from the whole Collections, half bound, uncut* 1820-22-23-25

1336 Zuallardo (G.) Viaggio di Gerusalemme, *portrait and plates by N. Bonifacio, vellum* *Roma,* 1587

FOLIO.

1337 Roma in 1878-79. A Collection of 64 large Engravings (*several coloured*), including Funeral of Victor Emanuel II, Portrait and Oath of Humbert I, Portrait of his Queen, Portrait of Pius IX lying on his Death-Bed and in State, and Funeral, Italian Alliance, the Conclave, Portrait of Leo XIII and his Coronation, Cardinal Pecci, Ceremony of the Garter, Abraham and Hagar, Leo XIII al Bivio, Scenes Al Vaticano, Friggitoria Romana, L'Allocuzione, Attempt to assassinate Humbert I and after Arrival in Rome, La Grisi, On the Bridge, La Valanga, Carneval, Ballet, Modern Fables, First Baking, Concorso per Roma, Primavera, &c. &c. from the Don Pirloncino, Osservatore Romano, Voce della Verita, &c. *half calf*   *Roma*, 1878-79

1338 Rome in 1878. A Collection of Cuttings from English, French and Italian Newspapers, *portrait of Leo XIII and a few other plates added, pasted in an album*

1339 Rossi (G.) Pitture a Fresco del Camposanto di Pisa, *engravings by G. P. Lasinio, half bound, uncut*   *Firenze*, 1832

1340 RUSKIN (J.) FRESCOES OF GIOTTO, 38 *engravings, with explanatory Notices in royal 8vo,* 2 vol. *half red morocco, uncut, top edges gilt*   1854-60

1341 Seneca Moralis (Opera), *several leaves damaged and mended, sold with all faults, russia, gilt edges*   *Venetiis*, 1490

1342 SIDONII APOLLINARIS POEMA AUREUM ejusdemque Epistolæ, FIRST EDITION WITH A DATE, *half blue morocco*   *Mediolani, U. Scinzenzeler*, 1498

 ** Extremely rare. The Roxburghe copy sold for £12 12s.

1343 Simonides (C.) Facsimiles of certain Portions of the Gospel of St. Matthew and of the Epistles of St. James and St. Jude, written on Papyrus in the first Century, with Notes and Prolegomena   1862

1344 SOLINUS DE SITU ET MEMORABILIBUS ORBIS, FIRST EDITION, *fine copy in blue morocco extra, gilt edges, by C. Lewis*   *Venetiis, N. Jenson*, 1473

 ** Scarce. The Pinelli copy sold for £10 and Heber's for £11 11s.

1345 Spence (J.) Polymetis, FIRST EDITION, *portrait and plates (including the suppressed portrait of Provost Cooke with donkey's head), old calf*   1747

1346 Spruner (K. von) Historico-geographical Atlas, 26 *coloured plates*   1861

1347 SUETONIUS DE VITA CÆSARUM, *very large copy* (11¾ by 7⅝ *inches), but unfortunately having first leaf in facsimile, calf extra*   *Venetiis, N. Jenson,* 1471

  *** Extremely rare. The Sunderland copy, not so large, sold for £27.

1348 SUIDÆ LEXICON, Græce, FIRST EDITION, *old green morocco, gilt edges*   *Mediolani, D. Chalcondylas,* 1499

  *** Scarce. Dr. Askew's copy sold for £8 8s.

1349 Suidæ Lexicon, Gr. post L. Kusterum ad Codices MSS. recensuit T. Gaisford cum Indicibus, 3 vol. *portrait of Gaisford added, russia extra*   *Oxonii,* 1834

1350 Surplice (The), a Journal of Ecclesiastical Affairs, from 29 November 1845 to 26 September 1846 inclusive, *woodcuts, half calf gilt*   1845-46

1351 Taciti Libri V noviter inventi atque cum reliquis ejus Operibus editi Cura P. Beroaldi, *MS. notes, very large copy in calf*   *Romæ, S. Guilleretus,* 1515

  *** This very rare edition ranks amongst Editiones Principes, on account of containing Books I to V of Annals for the first time. Sir J. Thorold's copy sold for £10 5s.

1352 Tanner (Bp. T.) Notitia Monastica, with Additions by J. Nasmith, BEST EDITION, *portrait and plates of arms, russia extra*   *Cambridge,* 1787

1353 Tennyson (A.) Guinevere and Vivien, 2 vol. *illustrations by G. Doré, ornamented cloth, gilt edges*   1867

1354 TERENTIANUS MAURUS DE LITTERIS, SYLLABIS, ET METRIS HORATII, *sheet* a *reprinted, sold with all faults, vellum*   *Mediolani,* 1497

  *** First edition, of extraordinary rarity. This copy on 27 October, 1803, sold for £9. See cutting from Athenæum respecting its rarity prefixed.

1355 TERENTIUS cum Directorio, Glosa interlineali et Commentariis, *numerous woodcuts, fine copy in red morocco extra, gilt edges, by C. Smith*
    Urbe Argentina, J. Grüninger, 1496

  *** Very Scarce. In the Bibliotheca Spenceriana Dr. Dibdin has allotted 12 pages to the description of this edition.

1356 Testamentum Novum Græcum cum Commentario J. J. Wetstenii, 2 vol. *old calf*   *Amst.* 1751-52

  *** At end of vol. II is added: " Duæ Epistolæ S. Clementis Romani, Syriace et Latine edente J. J. Wetstenio, *Lugd. Bat.* 1752."

1357 THEOCRITI ECLOGÆ, Genus Theocriti, Catonis Sententiæ, Sententiæ septem Sapientum, de Invidia, Theognidis Sententiæ, Sententiæ Monastichi, Aurea Carmina Pythagoræ, Phocylidæ Poema, Carmina Sibyllæ Erythræeæ de Christo, Differentia Vocis, et Hesiodi Theogonia, Scutum Herculis atque Georgica. Omnia Græce, FIRST ALDINE EDITION *and first of most of the authors, very fine copy in red morocco extra, leather joints, silk linings, vellum fly-leaves, gilt edges, by Simier*
Venetiis, Aldus, 1495
*** This copy sold for £8 10s. in Sir J. Thorold's sale.

1358 Theocritus, &c. SECOND EDITION *of the Aldine issue, russia extra, leather joints, gilt edges, by C. Hering,* ib. 1495
Very rare. Sir M. Sykes's copy sold for £13 13s.

1359 THUCYDIDES, Græce Cura Aldi Manutii, FIRST EDITION, *Bp. Blomfield's copy, with his book-plate, first 2 leaves mended, sold with all faults, old red morocco, gilt edges*
ib. 1502
*** Very scarce. Wodhull's copy sold for £15.

1360 Tuer (A. W.) Luxurious Bathing, *with 12 folio etchings, initials, &c. by Sutton Sharpe, Proofs on Japanese paper, half vellum, parchment sides* 1879

1361 UGHELLI (F.) ITALIA SACRA aucta Cura N. Coleti, 10 vol. in 7, BEST EDITION, *coats of arms, half vellum, uncut*
Venetiis, 1717-22

1362 Utino (Leonardi de) Quadragesimale aureum, *stained and several leaves mended, sold with all faults, vellum*
(*ib.*) 1471

1363 Vænii (O.) Vita D. Thomæ Aquinatis, 30 *plates, Antverpiæ,* 1610—Vita S. Rosæ de Peru, 40 *plates (wanting 34 and 35) ib. s. a.*—Vita S. Mariæ Magdalenæ de Pazzis, 50 *plates, ib. s. a.*—Eleven Landscapes by A. Perelle, *fine impressions, calf* in 1 *vol.*
*** This copy sold for £3 3s. in Mr. Beckford's sale.

1364 WHARTON (H.) ANGLIA SACRA sive Collectio Historiarum de Archiepiscopis et Episcopis Angliæ ad Annum 1540, 2 vol. LARGE PAPER, *old calf* 1691
*** Scarce on Large Paper. Hanrott's copy sold for £8 8s.

1365 Wood (A. à) Historia et Antiquitates Universitatis Oxoniensis, 2 vol. in 1, *frontispiece, with plate of costume and plan of Oxford added* Oxonii, 1674

1366 Xenophontis Opera, Græce, Cura E. Bonini, FIRST EDITION, *fine copy in brown morocco extra, gilt edges*
Florentiæ, P. Junta, 1516
*** Very scarce. Sir J. Thorold's copy sold for £4 11s.

Dryden Press: J. DAVY & SONS, 137, Long Acre, London.

BAKER, LEIGH & SOTHEBY.

THE FIRM COMMENCING WITH SAMUEL BAKER IN

1744.

SOTHEBY, WILKINSON & HODGE.
1891.

www.ingramcontent.com/pod-product-compliance
Ingram Content Group UK Ltd.
Pitfield, Milton Keynes, MK11 3LW, UK
UKHW042150280225
455719UK00001B/250